STANISLAW LEM

Liverpool Science Fiction Texts and Studies, 46

Liverpool Science Fiction Texts and Studies

Editor David Seed, *University of Liverpool*

Editorial Board
Mark Bould, *University of the West of England*
Veronica Hollinger, *Trent University*
Rob Latham, *University of California*
Roger Luckhurst, *Birkbeck College, University of London*
Patrick Parrinder, *University of Reading*
Andy Sawyer, *University of Liverpool*

Recent titles in the series

22. Inez van der Spek *Alien Plots: Female Subjectivity and the Divine*
23. S. T. Joshi *Ramsey Campbell and Modern Horror Fiction*
24. Mike Ashley *The Time Machines: The Story of the Science-Fiction Pulp Magazines from the Beginning to 1950*
25. Warren G. Rochelle *Communities of the Heart: The Rhetoric of Myth in the Fiction of Ursula K. Le Guin*
26. S. T. Joshi *A Dreamer and a Visionary: H. P. Lovecraft in his Time*
27. Christopher Palmer *Philip K. Dick: Exhilaration and Terror of the Postmodern*
28. Charles E. Gannon *Rumors of War and Infernal Machines: Technomilitary Agenda-Setting in American and British Speculative Fiction*
29. Peter Wright *Attending Daedalus: Gene Wolfe, Artifice and the Reader*
30. Mike Ashley *Transformations: The Story of the Science-Fiction Magazine from 1950–1970*
31. Joanna Russ *The Country You Have Never Seen: Essays and Reviews*
32. Robert Philmus *Visions and Revisions: (Re)constructing Science Fiction*
33. Gene Wolfe (edited and introduced by Peter Wright) *Shadows of the New Sun: Wolfe on Writing/Writers on Wolfe*
34. Mike Ashley *Gateways to Forever: The Story of the Science-Fiction Magazine from 1970–1980*
35. Patricia Kerslake *Science Fiction and Empire*
36. Keith Williams *H. G. Wells, Modernity and the Movies*
37. Wendy Gay Pearson, Veronica Hollinger and Joan Gordon (eds.) *Queer Universes: Sexualities and Science Fiction*
38. John Wyndham (eds. David Ketterer and Andy Sawyer) *Plan for Chaos*
39. Sherryl Vint *Animal Alterity: Science Fiction and the Question of the Animal*
40. Paul Williams *Race, Ethnicity and Nuclear War: Representations of Nuclear Weapons and Post-Apocalyptic Worlds*
41. Sara Wasson and Emily Alder, *Gothic Science Fiction 1980–2010*
42. David Seed (ed.), *Future Wars: The Anticipations and the Fears*
43. Andrew M. Butler, *Solar Flares: Science Fiction in the 1970s*
44. Andrew Milner, *Locating Science Fiction*
45. Joshua Raulerson, *Singularities*

STANISLAW LEM

Selected Letters to Michael Kandel

EDITED, TRANSLATED
AND WITH AN INTRODUCTION BY
PETER SWIRSKI

LIVERPOOL UNIVERSITY PRESS

First published 2014 by
Liverpool University Press
4 Cambridge Street
Liverpool
L69 7ZU

Copyright © Stanislaw Lem 1972–1987
Copyright © Barbara and Tomasz Lem 2014

All rights reserved. No part of this book may be reproduced, stored in a retrieval system, or transmitted, in any form or by any means, electronic, mechanical, photocopying, recording, or otherwise, without the prior written permission of the publisher.

British Library Cataloguing-in-Publication data
A British Library CIP record is available

ISBN 978-1-78138-017-8 cased

Typeset by Carnegie Book Production, Lancaster
Printed and bound by Booksfactory.co.uk.

Contents

Introduction	1
Selected Letters, 1972–1987	5
Stanislaw Lem Chronology	165
Index of Names and Titles	167

Dedicated to:

Stanislaw Lem
Barbara Lem
Tomasz Lem

> Not knowing what lies ahead,
> I write in order to find out a little about it.
> Stanislaw Lem

Introduction

Stanislaw Lem died on 26 March 2006. No one can bring his mortal engine back to life, but in this book his voice can be heard afresh for the benefit of all those who believe that, with his passing, a quintessential element of twentieth-century artistic and intellectual heritage has come to an end. The following translation of his selected letters is the medium of this resurrection and I am its necromancer.

Translations may be, as Borges aphorized, like wives: the more beautiful, the less faithful. In his lifetime Lem favoured only three translators: his best German-language translator, Irmtraud Zimmerman Göllheim; Michael Kandel, nominated for the National Book Award for his work of *The Cyberiad* and other fictions; and myself, who earned thumbs up for the translations of our interviews from the 1990s that form the core of *A Stanislaw Lem Reader* (1997) as well as of sundry essays, including the one fronting *The Art and Science of Stanislaw Lem* (2006).

What follows is my annotated translation of Lem's fifteen-year correspondence with Michael Kandel, his principal American translator. The first letter below dates from 1972, a year in-between *A Perfect Vacuum* and *Imaginary Magnitude*. The last one dates from 1987, the year of the Polish edition of *Peace on Earth* and *Fiasco*. Afterward, sporadic as it had long become before that stage, the exchanges between the writer and the translator peter out altogether. All together, they offer an unparalleled testimony to Lem's raw intellectual powers, smouldering literary passions, and abiding personal concerns from the central period of his life and career. In the process they open never-before-seen polemical vistas on writing, literature, translation, philosophy, science, politics, culture—and, not least, his personal life.

Yes, personal, for even as they reposition Lem as a consummate litterateur and an intellectual oracle, the letters reveal tantalizing glimpses of the man behind the giant. Scathing in criticism, generous in praise, prescient in prognoses, a master of the art of provocation, the letters lift the veil not only on his creative process but sometimes on the intimate, even painful, side of life in Poland. Fighting depression, at times hitting the bottle, plagued by ill health, obsessed by his legacy, driven to distraction by lack of appreciation in the United States, Lem the arch-rationalist emerges here at his most human, vulnerable, and... likeable.

Translation is a tricky business at any time, and trickier still when the editor must decide *which* words and opinions to translate. After all, even if many of Lem's letters elevate the epistolary to an art form, not all are, at the end of the day, of equal interest. What you see before you, then, is *my* Lem resurrected from a stack of correspondence an inch thick.

Here is what got left on the cutting room floor. "Our Collected Letters may one day turn out to be an encyclopedic prolegomenon to the Theory of Translation", joked the writer on 23 August 1972, and for a good reason. Page after page, Lem dispenses nuts-and-bolts advice on how best to render his prose into English in passages that demand punctilious knowledge of the exact phrasing of the stories in question—too exact, for the most part, to sustain the attention of readers who are not themselves practitioners or theoreticians of the *metier*. A representative selection of Lem's encyclopedic prolegomenon that you will find below is, in other words, just that: a representative selection.

The bulk of omissions, however comprise Lem's countless, not to say obsessive, invocations of FAME & FORTUNE (virtually always cast in BLOCK TYPE). It quickly becomes commonplace, then tiresome, to follow the twists and turns of his strategizing, proposing, disposing, backtracking, and double-guessing himself in his unrequited quest to make a splash on the other side of the Atlantic—to which more than once he professes utter indifference, only to return to it, like a homing pigeon, again, and again... and again.

There is something endearing to this side of Lem, wealthy and famous beyond what he had ever hoped for (as he himself concedes), yet fervently hoping to make it big in America—not so much, it must be said, for the sake of hitting pay dirt but for the sake of communicating what he believed in more than anything else in his life: a vision of the future present conjured up by his extraordinary imagination and hard-nosed intellect. Still, most of this shop-talk had to go by the wayside, or else you'd be reading a book the size of New York City's white pages (and of equal interest).

In the opening pages of *One Human Minute*, for no apparent reason other than to vent his spleen, Lem takes a detour to complain about book publishers. Anyone who has ever published a book will find comfort in his characteristically unflinching verdict: publishers suck. Unprofessional, brain-dead, lazy, incompetent, lacking even a modicum of aesthetic and intellectual (common) sense, his portrait of men and women who publish books for a living could hardly be more accusatory and devastating.

The entire passage could have been taken verbatim from the letters, so many of which drip with acid mixed with derision for the profession that, after all, enabled Lem to make his living. But, much like his periodic philippics—whether couched in terms of statistics, cybernetics, aesthetic theory, or literary history—against the cultural booboisie incapable of separating visionary art from commercial pap, once you've read one, you've read them all. What you will see below is thus a pale ghost of what had to be left behind.

Ditto when it comes to pages upon pages of boosting, cajoling, browbeating, retreating, confessing, thundering, apologizing, and rhetorizing in an effort to coax the best and the most out of his American translator. Lem the Perfectionist keeps moving the goalpost in keeping with the Polish saying that 'appetite grows as you eat'—even as, at the same time, he remains self-critical to a fault. Literature and art are his supreme arbiters, not unlike Faulkner who was willing to sacrifice his mother on the altar of art (as Lem's letters reveal, he dutifully tended to his parents and mother-in-law).

Finally, a note on typography. Given how often Lem forswore command of English, it is nothing short of astonishing to see how often he breaks into that language in letters to his English-speaking correspondents, to which I can attest from experience. How often? Since in the letters below Polish and English sentences stand side by side in the same type, to bring out the contrast, every word that Lem wrote in English is set **in bold type**, transcribed verbatim, no matter ungrammatical or missspeld.

In general, I made every effort to render Lem's thoughts and thought processes as faithfully as possible, even in typography. To wit: All Capitalized Words, ALL BLOCK WORDS, <u>all underlines</u> and *italics*, "all quotations marks", all multiple question marks???, all exclamation points!, all regular ellipses... and all paragraph breaks are Lem's. Yes—the marathon paragraphs are all without exception his, no matter how much one might wish to dice them up into more digestible chunks. Similarly, almost all sentence breaks are Lem's, except when non-sequiturs and seemingly stream-of-consciousness lurches sideways were too much to wrap one's head around.

Throughout I tried to preserve all references to projects that Lem was either in the throes of writing or else trying out for size, before apparently letting them fall off the face of the earth, only to resurrect them sometimes long years after the magnesium flash of the original idea.

Selected Letters, 1972–1987

Translated and annotated by Peter Swirski

Cracow, 1 February 1972

[...]

I am undoubtedly one of the few people in Poland currently enjoying a measure of fame in the East and starting to acquire some renown in the West. Because of everything that this country has gone through, it is now regrettably sub-par in matters of culture. As a consequence it lacks an established sense of intellectual independence, so much so that, as soon as somebody in New York or Bonn[1] or Rome calls me outstanding, everyone over here drops to his knees post-haste. As for me, in the fiftieth year of my life, god knows I could hardly care less. I care about being able to continue working — and, I admit, not to have to wait till after my death to see my concepts "shine". (Summa technologiae already came out in the USSR; now it's coming out in Hungary, and there are realistic prospects for West Germany).

Two more things. Sure, I know Calvino's Cosmicomics; it's not bad, but for some reason does not appeal to me (I can appreciate the originality but can't warm up to the whole thing). Also, I must confess I'm quite disappointed with the entirety of American science fiction, not excluding Asimov. To my mind, he puts "super" back in "superficiality": his literary works grossly simplify the entire scientific

---

[1] Then the capital of West Germany.

paradigm. Asimov the biochemist KNOWS a hell of a lot more than Asimov the writer.

Anyway, I don't mean to belabour the point; instead, I'd better send you the latest edition of The Star Diaries in which I'd like to draw your attention to the (new) Twenty-First Voyage as an example of a story in which my "metaphysical convictions" come clearly to the fore. Above all, science fiction occupies a ground blighted by a simply unbelievable amount of hyped-up trash — it covers cognitive problems with so much trash that they disappear from sight. I don't see, by the way, any chance of reversing this convoluted trend since this is not a task for any individual, not even Dostoyevsky and Einstein combined (I do not see myself as either the former or the latter — not out of false modesty but for categorically different reasons: cognizance of my own powers and limitations).

I would also like to send you Science Fiction and Futurology, my Hammer on SF, even though, as I wrote in the afterword, the annihilation of science fiction was never my original intention. That study is in some sense a continuation of The Philosophy of Chance. Nowadays I'm wrestling with a new book — I've been at it for a long time, only I just don't know how to write it since I took on myself to create something that, in truth, cannot be written at all. (The title is going to be Golem XIV; the whole thing, devoid of any action, is supposed to be a stenography of a series of discussions about everything under the sun — and a bunch of other things besides — conducted at MIT by various groups of scientists with a certain Supercomputer at the end of the 20th century).

The Computer was built in the Third Phase of the arms race, i.e., during the escalation of construction of strategic digital automata. Inordinate efforts on the part of the constructors created, at the cost of several billion dollars, a machine that doesn't give a damn about military strategy, devoting itself entirely to questions of ontology, instead.

Well, I'm glad I got to know you through correspondence at least. Too bad you didn't get in touch when in Poland for I'm far from the ogre that, I know, I'm made out to be. Life, to put it simply, is way too short for chewing the fat and shooting the breeze.

[...]

Another thing is that it is, indeed, difficult to classify me or to extract my beliefs from my belletristic works. Cybernetics created a certain framework of concepts which I "inhabited" for some time but, at the end of the day, it was far from anything like my final "anchorage". After the "cybernetic period" I got more closely acquainted with structural linguistics as well as with other less hermeneutic types of structuralism (I'm thinking here of the French school — Levi Strauss, et alii). Naturally, there is nothing to stop you from isolating a certain leitmotif in my works and pursuing it. My views on literary theory are delineated in The Philosophy of Chance, admittedly in a rather laborious and complicated manner because of the resistance of the material which I had not completely mastered by the time I sat down to write about it, so that the process of writing became at the same time a process of self-education. I developed some aspects of that study much more clearly and concisely in the first volume of Science Fiction and Futurology. In my conception, a literary work is a MODEL, and the investigator's task is to determine a set of processes characteristic of the work and/or of processes related to it.

Our Institute of Literary Studies organized a discussion of The Philosophy of Chance — I'll be glad to send you an offprint of these talks since some things in there are presented very clearly indeed. What is quite specific in my case is that I am at once a theorist and a practitioner of literature. This double identity stood me in good stead during the composition of A Perfect Vacuum.

By the way, I cannot claim that I fully cracked the key problematics of a literary work, such as the issues relating to the formalist foundations of semantic polyvalence or to the function of logical contradictions, antinomies, and paradoxes (in terms of formal logic). I've no doubt that my theoretical studies would profit a great deal if I could write them <u>all over again</u>, but for basic biological reasons (rather than out of laziness, I hope) I can't afford to do that.

[...]

****

Cracow, 26 February 1972

[...]

<u>His Master's Voice</u> was written to simulate at various points having been translated from the English, which does not mean, of course, that this ought to make the actual English translation any easier! As for the vocabulary, I'm not denying that it is at times technical, but that has never been much of a problem for me since, generally speaking, I know English as well as Polish or even better within the narrow range of disciplinary penetration... or when Polish equivalents simply do not exist (e.g., hardware-software). As far as your reservations go, it is completely unnecessary to tread on eggshells (I'm referring to the reservations aimed at my belletristic works). I'm not Mohammed or some other Messiah, and I've no need for a prophet or a John the Baptist. By all means, please apply yourself to the most intense critique you can muster — so long as it is deep-rooted and specific — and please don't hesitate to contradict me whenever you feel the material warrants it. As to how many elements in your rendition of my books

originate with you and how many with me, this is
a general problem that occupied me during the
composition of The Philosophy of Chance in which,
with complete deliberation and exaggeration, I
propounded iconoclastic theses that a literary work
is only a projection of possibilities, with the
definitive closure of the creative process occurring
only during interpretation. Works oscillate along
the axis of mutually opposed extremes of radical
determinism and radical indeterminism (think of the
opposition between Rorschach's test and a chemical
description of some complex molecule: the perceiver
projects "himself" maximally into the description
of Rorschach's inkblots but minimally into the
formal structure of the molecule). I approached this
problem mainly from a sociological perspective,
arguing that a "stabilizing reception" of a work
performs a function similar to that by means of
which (natural) selection stabilizes a species in
the course of evolution. Because of this, I don't
think there are true or false interpretations, only
ones that maximize or impoverish the "gestalt-
quality" of a work as a whole. The way in which
a reader integrates the work will regulate his
interpretation; this is his business and his perfect
right, sanctioned by the public opinion to the
extent that it has already performed a collective
act of interpretation (denotation, connotation)
— in other words, assigned a given work to its
ecological niche within an established system of
cultural norms, facts, qualities, values, etc.
From the empirical standpoint there is no other
alternative, since the dichotomy between truth and
falsehood does not obtain here. Naturally, there
is a purely intuitive commonsensical borderline
beyond which a singular interpretation of a work
ceases to be "normal" (albeit strongly individu-
alistic) and turns into a "pathological" reading,
i.e., into an excessive, aberrant departure from
the intentional (literal and indirect) denomi-
nators of meaning carried by the work. There is no
literary composition that could not be interpreted

in a multitude of ways: either as an expression of
the author's personality, or a cross-section of a
literary-cultural current of the era, or a certain
type of social conflict, and such like. No books,
including my own, can escape these strictures and
as such I must remain — even if I did not want to
— a radical liberal when it comes to the meaning
of what I create as a belletrist. Of course, I am
always aware of this "double-edged sword" in my
writings — of being trapped between the denotative
and the artistic mode of information.

All of my efforts have always been directed at
not repeating myself. For instance, I am working
at present on the next voyage of Ijon Tichy. The
story will depict twice over "the same" events on
a fictional planet: the first time what the observer
perceives strictly as a behaviourist — since his
"translator" is broken, he integrates everything
according to earthly concepts and imagery — and
only later, when the "translator" is repaired,
it becomes apparent that everything he saw was
completely different. Thus at first he beholds
monsters devouring and then vomiting one another —
bipedal and hemipedal creatures (Bihemes) capable
of agglutinating into enormous monstrums which,
in these horrific forms, feast on each other only
to end up puking afterwards — but, later on, all
this vomiting and upchucking reveals a higher
sense of essential personal and state development
in terms of the planet's culture (at the same time
conveying rather explicit allusions to all kinds
of subtexts). This propositional dimension can
be outlined easily, and the whole problem lies in
discovering the optimal conditions for solving the
puzzle narratively; in short, I'm talking about
modelling by trial and error which costs me a great
deal of energy, even though in this particular
case I know more or less what I need to do (and
how). The above example, which I would liken to the
general conception behind the tribe of Yahoos in
Swift, reveals perhaps most clearly what I particularly miss in SF. A modelling game of this sort

may take place simultaneously on many levels. There are countless thrillers in existence, but there was only one Father Brown; moreover, there are very few stories in the Father Brown series that meet the tacit conditions imposed by Chesterton's Catholicism without hammering a whole bunch of square facts into narrative round holes (to me, "The Man Who Was Thursday" is a very good example of a successful composition). I'd have nothing against reading potboilers if only they were gripping — I mean genuinely gripping — and if, like a pang of conscience, I was not oppressed by the awareness that the number of books anyone can read is finite, and that we are destined to leave this earth having undoubtedly missed on an abundance of valuable works and ideas, just because the sum total of our cultural heritage exceeds the capacity to absorb it in a lifetime. At the same time, I understand very well that not everybody dreams of this kind of life, balancing the time spent on every book against existential angst!

  Quite simply, in the light of the growing interest from academic circles in the U.S., SF criticism seems to me to be heading in a culturally perilous direction. It used to be about dreams of knocking down the walls of the literary ghetto from the outside insofar as the ghetto was incapable of liberating itself. Now pretty much uncritical apologias go hand in hand with "<u>Anschluss</u>" by means of which the inferior values of the ghetto are to be elevated and made respectable in the literary "mainstream" — all so that the ghetto should now encompass "all other" literature on the principle of equal rights, so pleasing to so many these days (by the same token, if all heterosexual practices are admissible, then so are all homosexual ones; if homosexual acts are ok, then why not necrophilic, so long as the persons legally looking after the corpses have no objections; and if necrophilic, then why not cannibalistic, so long as the consumee expresses a desire to be ingested, etc.). This levelling is in practice a slide into axiological nihilism. Culture cannot do without (**hill-climbing**) gradients, or else in practice it ends up levelling everything down, for, if everybody is equal, then truly no one can be more equal than others.

[...]

****

Cracow, 24 March 1972

[...]

You're right, my humour is infernal. That's the whole point — otherwise, I think, readers would be repelled. The icing sugar of a joke sweetens the pill at the moment of swallowing. Later on you're left with an aftertaste of bitterness that, I don't think I have to assure you, I did not invent myself, for it comes from the outside, i.e., from the world we live in. Yes: Dostoyevsky is perhaps the writer closest to me spiritually, even though this is intimacy with disease, mishap, hell, nightmare, and the spectre of a grave, rather than anything else. You can find quotations from Dostoyevsky, for example, in my <u>Dialogues</u> (from the confessions of The Underground Man). As for the hunger for the Absolute... I think I know this hunger, but personally I'm convinced that it can never be satisfied, since the Absolute <u>does not exist in a form that can be accepted</u>. In some ways, the sole Absolute, the sole model of God I can seriously accept, is God ∅. The Demolitians from Tichy's Twenty-First Voyage embody my personal view on faith, i.e., they were created with the utmost seriousness of which I'm at all capable. As for <u>The Philosophy of Chance</u>, it doesn't lack explicit warnings about what it ISN'T, in other words, what it omits to talk about — namely, practically the entire aesthetic domain (the dimension of experiencing a work aesthetically) — since my method is incapable of dealing with it. It's not merely question of differences of opinion — I was purposely silent on the subject I regard as wholly closed to analysis.[2]

Do I expect too much from Americans when it comes to Culture? Actually, I'd have to say that I don't expect much at all. Every time I wrote on the subject of science fiction, I trashed it as well as I could using all the skills and talents at my disposal, not even as a writer but above all as a chagrined, bored to death, disappointed, dumbed down reader. Recently I took a risk on a wider forum by replying in English to a Canadian fanzine which asked for my views on matters related to SF — if they publish my replies, I'll make sure they get into your hands insofar as they attest to my real convictions, even if lamely expressed. Your remarks about the value we in Poland attribute to culture seem to me highly paradoxical simply because so many people and initiatives here were destroyed after the war precisely for the opposite reason. At the same time, I perfectly understand that the subjectivity of the standards we use goes back to the history of our respective countries, for over here we were mortally imperilled (in the literal sense), first of all culturally but also biologically, whereas for the Americans the Apocalypse has never been more than a play of imagination — as opposed to reality, personally experienced.

[...]

The American Embassy in Poland has already twice offered me an opportunity to spend half a year or even longer in the United States, which I declined for various reasons, mainly for lack of time but also perhaps out of pride since, I confess, I'd

---

[2] Experiencing a work aesthetically is far from closed to analysis; see Swirski, *Literature, Analytically Speaking: Explorations in the Theory of Interpretation, Analytic Aesthetics, and Evolution* (2010).

prefer not to be an unknown quantity on arrival and have at least a few books out in the States to my credit. I am aware that, at the end of the day (Mann wrote about it at length, even though he was a Nobelist), a litterateur makes a comical and pathetic figure, especially a litterateur <u>anonyme</u> of whom no one knows a thing since no one has ever heard about his books. Not to put too fine a point on it, he becomes a figure of auto-parody.

[...]

****

Cracow, 26 April 1972

[...]

I have already written some French, Polish and German letters today, but not a single in English. So it is a temptation, to write you in this way — but an idiotic idea, too; so I shall switch my albuminous computer into his polish paths.

[...]

Thank you for the kind words regarding my son. He is doing better. My Tommy is four already. The responsibilities of fatherhood are not easy in our world!

It is funny that you found the English version of <u>Memoirs Found in the Bathtub</u> easier to digest than the original. Of course, this is Kafka, albeit run through Gombrowicz.

[...]

As for me, I'm incapable of translating even myself. I discovered this quite to my astonishment. I was asked to publish at home several pieces that

I had written in German, for the Germans, and I couldn't do it! Every language derives its traction and focus of expression from a different place! I would have to write from scratch in Polish on the same subject but, needless to say, in that case we're no longer talking about translation at all, so in the end I gave up. As for The Cyberiad, I cannot imagine a more difficult thing to translate in prose. Of course, it's a different story with poetry. Leśmian is utterly untranslatable outside the range of Slavic languages, and Rilke cannot be detached from his Germanness.

POST SCRIPTUM. **This letter was fished out from a heap of junk — I was SURE it is already flying above Atlantic — you see the point? The Chaos takes over — I am losing the last bit of the hope of an ultimate victory, i.e., the Entropy is rising.**

Now, even if I DO NOT speak English, I have already English dreams, i.e., insights into the Nature of Being. This came to my mind: if Information could have Mass, as Matter does, and Energy too, then the Mystery is Solved. The Lord's Countdown from Infinity to Zero made the World. It sounds good in English; alas, not so, when translated into my own language.

[...]

****

Cracow, 8 May 1972

[...]

It seems to me (since I've no means of knowing for sure) that certain virtues of The Cyberiad stem from a phenomenon I would call linguistic counterpoint — counterpoint that relies on a juxtaposition of different linguistic registers and different styles.

To wit: passages stylized archaically contain terminology from physics, and state-of-the-art physics at that (hussars who wield hand-lasers; the lasers are equipped with flintlocks; etc.). Thus the style partially contradicts the words: the words look askance at the archaic setting; this is essentially the basis of poetry ("words that look askance at themselves"). The point is that neither "side" should win over the other. The whole setup should ultimately lean neither toward physics nor toward archaism — the balance between the two, the oscillation, should persist. The result is a kind of readerly "irritation", and consequently a sensation of comedy (rather than, of course, irritation).

"Hear then, noble sirs, the history of Zipperupus, king of the Partheginians, the Deutons, and the Profligoths, of whom concupiscence was the ruin".[3]
a) the invocation is taken from Tristan and Isolde.
b) Zipperupus[4] is Theodoric crossed with a pants' zipper. c) I turned Ostrogoths into Profligoths[...][5]
d) Deutons are straight from physics: deuterons, etc.[...]

Naturally, if I were to compose analytically in this way, with a dictionary in hand, I'd never write a single book in my life. Instead, all these things rattled somehow in and out of my fiendish cranium.

What can I suggest in the way of advice?
a) idioms from modern strategy, so beloved by the Pentagon (from which I cooked up **MOUSE — Minimal Orbital Unmanned Satellite, Earth**; all kinds of Eniacs, Geniacs, etc.); **MIRVs (Multiple Independent Reentry Vehicle)**; **ICPM** (that's me, **Intercontinental Philosophical Missile**); **second strike capability,** etc. Are you up to date with this rarefied terminology? It hides enormous possibilities in terms of the grotesque! b) slang, of course.

---

[3] From "Tale of the Three Storytelling Machines of King Genius" from *The Cyberiad*.
[4] "Rozporyk" in the original; in Polish "rozporek" means "pants' zipper".
[5] Lem's brief explanations of the etymology of his Polish neologisms lack English equivalents ("Profligoths", for example, is a free translation that departs from the Polish).

c) something that acts as a comprehensive frame of reference, only I've no idea what: for a French writer of historical novels it would be Dumas, for a Pole it would be Sienkiewicz (side by side, he dwarfs Dumas linguistically). d) vocabulary from cybernetics and physics (they can be splintered: in other words, renewed idiomatically — **feedback, feed him back** — I'm not sure at the moment what exactly can be done with that but I can imagine a context in which it might work as a colloquialism rooted in a cybernetic term). e) LEGALESE — language of diplomatic notes, language of legal codices, constitutional language, etc. Let's not be afraid of nonsense! In the Steelypips[6] there is a mention of a Comet-in-a-bonnet, of course chiefly because of the rhyme and not out of any profound signification; analogically one can have **"Planet Janet"**, **"commentary cometary"**, and so on. Even a word inserted completely "by chance" becomes dominated by the context and starts to perform the function of a local embellishment or "curiosum". Next, contaminations (**strange — estrangement** — if there were a way to hitch it to **"strangulation"**, it would be peachy). Anyway, how should I know!

On the margin: certain parts of Memoirs Found in a Bathtub were composed in blank verse (the conversation between the priest and the hero after the wild party). For the most part the rhythm carries the thing quite well, but the phrasing mustn't be forced too hard, I know that much.

Defects can arise out of a deliberate intensification of virtues (**cometary commentary about a weary cemetery**). I'm sharing all this with you since audacity takes a while to spread its wings. Brashness, even brazenness, is indispensable at this point (linguistically speaking, of course). It is possible to demonstrate this by comparing the somewhat "timid" Robotic Fables with The Cyberiad, or the first part of The Cyberiad with the second, which shows a higher degree of immoderation.

---

[6] "The Fifth Sally (A)" from *The Cyberiad*.

(N.B., I made for myself long lists of words beginning with "cyb-cyber-ceber" and I researched roots of "ber" to manufacture "**cyberberine**" from "**berberine**", etc.). Other possibilities: "**Cyberserker**", "**cyberhyme**", although they don't sound as good as in Polish. (Anyway, I've got no ear for it). One can also collage phrases from "trash" (excerpts from contemporary pop "hits", nursery rhymes, sayings, contaminating all without mercy).

[...]

****

Cracow, 30 May 1972

[...]

Well, I will be glad to countenance any and all forms of interest in my writing, only I really do not speak and do not understand spoken English — I can only read and write, like a deaf-mute. I never studied English, I only read things with a dictionary in hand already during the occupation. Recently I even penned a few short essays in English on the same principle as the joke in which they ask Meyer if he can play the violin, and he replies, I don't know, never tried yet. So I tried it.

   Hogarth.[7] Well, putting it simply, he was ashamed of himself. He reckoned that he knew himself well, but the old saying is true, scratch a rationalist and watch an irrationalist bleed. He was aware that he found pleasure in other people's misery and because of that he did not trust himself. Generally speaking, real sinners feel quite good about themselves; only those who, in the final count, didn't do anything quite so terrible are plagued by conscience, for these things don't correlate

---

[7] Protagonist of *His Master's Voice*.

at all. It's amusing that in belles lettres — I'm not even thinking of SF — scientists are fenced off by a tight veil of silence, as if they were a separate species. Some of them are saintly, like Einstein, but others are monsters, and god forbid they should ever wield power over the world. I'm actually thinking of writing a pasquil on Einstein (naturally, not as a vie romancée,[8] but using him secretly as a model), I think it would be exceptionally interesting. He was a tragic figure in every sense, since everything for which he became famous had come about in his twenties and then for half a century he plugged away at a complete dead end (unified field theory), yet never stopped believing that he was right since "God does not play dice with the universe". I'd be curious to know if he ever called his wife by a wrong name. I mean, he was such an unbelievably fair-minded, magnanimous, and sensibly normal man that you can't but get suspicious...

I've a lot of sympathy for Hogarth. Not to harbour illusions can be a crushing thing, so maybe he worked out for himself a bit of an escape hatch. And Baloyne is my friend, a famous Polish critic who instantly recognized himself in the character...[9] I put more people from real life into that novel because I found it amusing (not Rappaport; him I created out of thin air).

[...]

****

---

[8] French: biographical novel.
[9] Jan Błoński (1931–2010), literary critic and professor at Jagiellonian University.

Zakopane, 9 June 1972

[...]

Specifically, Stalin's times concocted a myth, never concretely or cogently expressed, of the state as a machine that was not only perfect, but also omniscient and omnipotent — a machine whose functional magnificence, even as it ground people into dust, exhibited the beauty of a higher perfection of absolute evil. Opponents, enemies, humanists, all were equally awed by this triumphant perfection. The faith in it was responsible, for instance, for the notorious ease with which "confessions of guilt" were obtained at various trials. It had absolutely nothing to do with the version of Stalinism — to simplify things here a little — popularized by Orwell in 1984. The state functionary who tells O'Brien[10] that the future is a boot forever stamping on a human face is a totally unreal and fake figure. No representative of the regime was EVER such a Mephistopheles, a Machiavelli, a de Sade. Instead, there was the myth, more potent than any individual — and its unspoken evil beauty. Once shattered, nothing could ever put it back together again, and this is precisely why we are talking about faith, because absolute faith, once shattered, vanishes absolutely — all that's left behind is a void. At the end of the day, of course, nothing like this extraordinary and absolute evil was ever there. A hodgepodge of social phenomena, too complicated to disentangle here even by way of a simple classification, precipitated the emergence of that faith. Memoirs Found in a Bathtub is a document of those times. The Building[11] isn't perfect at all. The fact that FROM THE VERY OUTSET the protagonist can gallivant wherever he wants to around the Building, that he

---

[10] Lem is in error: it is O'Brien who speaks these words to Winston Smith.
[11] The plot takes place inside the headquarters of the Third Pentagon, aka the Building.

can enter secret or forbidden areas, view secret mobilization plans, etc., the fact that he sees the total cretinism and folly of the highest overlords of the Building, such as Kashenblade, is neither an accident nor any kind of narrative "letting go" nor inconsistency on my part. Whoever was close to the bigwigs of the regime could see their shabbiness but still continue to believe in the already mentioned perfection of the system. The myth draped itself in History with such extraordinary efficacy that it enslaved everyone — it seemed that History itself had morphed into this deranged and monstrous system from which there was no court of appeal. The Top Brass became a kind of mocking inversion of the image of God. In *Memoirs* the Building is not perfect, its perfection is only in the eye of the beholding protagonist who interprets logically, exactly, and precisely everything that happens to be accidental, mean, stupid, risible, jerry-rigged, unfinished, fragmentary in its existential mundaneness, so much so that he ascribes to the Building qualities it does not possess. Ordinary mess, disorder, chaos, downright shoddiness and mediocrity, unrecognized for what they are, become aggrandized and mystified and "identified" as symptoms of higher power and might — as Signs whose signification Must be absolute.

This type of behaviour on the part of the observer and participant in the events turns into a paranoid monomania. There are no accidents! Every man is transparent, defenceless, if even old men's facial moles constitute elements of state order. I would like to ask you to look at the book from this perspective. The whole machinery necessarily needed an appearance of being surrounded by terrible enemies since it marvellously justified the horrible methods used. The escalation of accusations and the deranged character of the alleged "guilt" — alleged anti-state activities — led to out-and-out absurdity (the notorious "milk cans" by means of which Jewish doctors were said to conduct assassinations of the highest state officials). This absurdity could be accepted <u>at face value</u> or else turned into a myth by believing in the perfection of the system — the only way that, by means of this unspoken secret, one could justify this order of things. It was this pervasive faith, I repeat, that was responsible for the helplessness and the inner emptiness of every person who attempted to resist being destroyed. The belief in the presence of ultimate evil rendered him absolutely empty inside. He had nothing <u>equally</u> ultimate in its nature to lean on in this contest. Only a person with a strongly internalized system of ABSOLUTE value was capable of resistance (e.g., someone authentically believing in God, as opposed to those practicing religion in an ordinary, tepid, indifferent way). It was in these circumstances that the idea of conformity, of willing acceptance of these utterly absurd accusations and charges — which were concocted, after all, out of hundred-percent lies — that the idea of internalizing these lies became a logical alternative. It is in this sense that it forms the narrative focus in my novel (the pact between the priest and the protagonist). Fight evil by filling the void of totally deceitful pronouncements with internally authentic content! And all this without any way of telling <u>externally</u> (i.e., behaviourally) the difference between guilt imposed by the executioner and guilt embraced Christ-like.

Because of these considerations, I regard the similarities between my book and the Kafkaesque paradigm as inconsequential and, frankly, accidental. I may sound boastful, like a frog that sticks out its leg when it's time to shoe horses, but let's not forget what different eras we're talking about. The jurisdiction of <u>The Trial</u> is, after all, a metaphor — it is anti-veridical, it is fictive, it is a trope for fate rather than any type of matrix for social relations, inasmuch as the entire tenor of the novel is para-sociological and metaphysical. Metaphysics as an autonomous theme does not feature in my book because the state devoured everything quite literally, factually, to the very end. I'm aware that readers who didn't experience the Stalinist system are unable to employ the latter as a paradigm to "test" the book, and that, in search of some such paradigm, per genus proximum et differentiam specificam[12] they eventually drift toward Kafka. As I said, there are two things that separate us. I mentioned the first: the faith that took root in the population as a response to the structural properties of existence under Stalinism. The other one is laughter which, as "wit", sits in a different place in Kafka. Kafka plays out his tragicomedies under a heaven that is certainly not empty; in my book, on the other hand, the penetration and domination by the state is such that any kind of faith refusing to accept the myth of absolute evil (itself coextensive with the social machine) — which is to say, faith in some form of Redemption, faith that would transcend reality — cannot even be articulated and communicated (as a message) in society. You can still have faith, but you can no longer confide it to another since there is no way to distinguish provocation from genuine Creed!

For the above reasons, I feel that you are not looking at the book the right way; then again, you lack the necessary experience which, as I said, has never been articulated — indeed, it was falsified on either side of the Curtain. Orwell correctly diagnosed certain peripheral symptoms but replaced faith in the supremacy of absolute evil with an admission from social-type Marquises de Sade who ostentatiously pronounce that the essence of their power is the orgasm that comes from destroying one individual after another. Nothing like that ever happened. All would-be elucidations lied at this point, being always lopsidedly entangled in the pragmatic tug-of-war between communists and anti-communists. No one looked for the truth but for a stick with which to clobber the opponent.

---

[12] Latin: "out of similarity and (common) differences".

I'm sitting here, writing a new booklet, provisionally titled The Mask.

[...]

****

Zakopane, 26 June 1972

[...]

On the subject of Memoirs Found in a Bathtub, I think I want to polemicize with you not for the sake of the book — I don't care for that — but for the sake of the truth. Memoirs is more realistic in spirit than you perhaps allow. It stems from a conception of state produced by Stalinism, probably the first type of system in history permeated by a very strong belief in the Absolute, albeit one located entirely in the present life. Please note that a logical analysis of the New Testament gives evidence of all kinds of contradictions and even manifest nonsense which, nota bene, drove some theologians to surmise that Jesus was a paranoiac. The cursing of the fig tree, for one, is completely gratuitous since figs in Palestine are out of season at the time when Jesus blighted one with his curse — wrong time of the year! But credenti non fit injuria.[13] Faith manifests itself, among others, in transposing all prima facie antinomies or paralogies from the ledger of "ought to" to "is".[14] I must stress that the version of Stalinism popularized in the West by Orwell and his imitators is a false rationalization. Take the key scene in 1984 when the state official tells O'Brien that the future is a boot stamping on a human face —

---

[13] Latin: "to a believer, no injury is done"; Lem puts the same words in the mouth of Father Arago in *Fiasco*.
[14] The basis of the so-called moralistic fallacy.

forever.[15] This is a two-bit demonism. The reality was much worse because it was never so consistent. More like, it was indifferent, replete with seediness, wastefulness, disorder, shambles, almost universal chaos — yet faith still attributed all this to the ledger of "is". An example from my novel is a scene in which the protagonist interprets moles on some old coot as signs attesting to the omniscience of the System that holds him in his power. After all, once you assume that such perfection EXISTS, you see it everywhere, and from then on all the mess, nonsense, claptrap is no longer what it is, namely chaotic tattiness, but becomes instead a Mystery, a Secret which — faith prompts us — we see only through a glass darkly and hence are unable to comprehend. It was precisely such faith and not any kind of torture that led the accused to confess to the most absurd acts during the infamous trials. They would "pull out all the stops" in affirming the charges levelled against them. Torture is one thing, but not everybody can be broken that way; we who survived the German occupation know a thing or two about it. Then we fought an enemy whose power was incomparably greater but who could be opposed in terms of inner values. But faced with History in the mantle of evil God (in the mantle of ineluctable social determinism), no one was in a position to defend his beliefs since no one was in a position to counter this mysterious absolute power with an even more powerful set of values — unless you were someone profoundly believing in divine transcendence. In that situation, however, your act of faith would have been restricted to an internal monologue or to a dialogue with the supposed God since there was no other way to express your faith — for the simple reason, attested in Memoirs, that an act of provocation was indistinguishable from an act of faith. Pseudo-teleological academies coaching how to imitate such faith and then designating chaplains (as part of the

---

[15] Lem reiterates his error from the preceding letter: the state official *is* O'Brien.

process of preventive espionage, i.e., infiltration of the clergy by graduates of such "institutes") are no fib. In sum, this absolute creed towered above any individual, no matter what his beliefs; Orwell was simply unable either to comprehend it or to find a place for it — and as such to convey it — in his novel. The completeness of human solitude stemmed from the fact that you could not trust anybody at all — in a transcendental (i.e., theological) sense, rather than in pragmatic terms of socio-psychology or of patterns of behaviour ingrained, for instance, in spies trained for action in enemy territory! It was Absolute Myth all the way, and when it collapsed, it collapsed absolutely too, leaving nothing behind except the amazement of the believers how their collective symptoms of this paranoid madness could have ever come about. These are facts and not phantasmagorias.

  I dare claim, dear Sir, that as a referent Kafka does not make sense here at all. After all, _The Trial_ fabricated the entire structure of jurisprudence; Kafka was a lawyer and knew well the working of the Austro-Hungarian justice system. He was not interested in social issues and the dissolution of society from _la belle époque_ allowed him this manoeuvre... so he went after ontology, abandoning the social dimension — in those days these domains were very clearly separated. In truth, only Dostoyevsky can be of some help here since only in him can you find a measure of understanding how it's at all possible that somebody falsely accused voluntarily internalizes the accusation, even though he can certainly gain nothing from it. The socio-psychological character of the mechanism that perpetrated such aberrations cannot be summarized in just a few words. The reflex desire of citizens under Stalinism was to become nothing and nobody, i.e., acquire a nondescript greyness by means of which to blend into the crowd, for only renunciation of all individual traits, it seemed, could save you... it was a common reflex, not at all grounded in any intellectual considerations. All this explains

the nondescriptness of my protagonist. He wanted to
be of service! He wanted to believe! He wanted to do
everything that was demanded of him, but the whole
dilemma is that the system didn't demand things
that people are authentically capable of. Please
kindly re-read the last sentence. Do you understand
what it says? Social reality became so perplexing,
so impenetrable, so full of secrets that nothing
but an act of completely irrational faith could
still integrate it and make it bearable — faith
that there is an explanation, that there is a way
to rationalize all this, only we little people don't
have the right to participate in this revelation. Of
course, there was no revelation of any kind, except
for the reality of strictly structural correlations
and a progression of historical phases of a newborn
system through successive phases — it's just that
this march was nobody's Machiavellian plot. There
was never anybody there so evil as Beelzebub
himself. The perception of diabolism as the first
principle and as the central plan was a complete
misunderstanding by people in the West — like
Orwell, who tried to rationalize the whole thing,
even though there was nothing to rationalize. In a
way, it was like being told to become like Jesus.
You practice walking on water every morning and
just can't understand why, even though you've done
everything by the book for twenty years, you still
sink as soon as you take the first step. The demands
of the state were impossible to meet, impossible
even to take literally, and yet supposedly that was
the way in which they were to be taken. Hence all
the nonsense in Orwell, insofar as he assumed that
all this stemmed from satanic premeditation. There
was no such perfect premeditation at all. Hence the
two totally contradictory images of the system: a
clay-legged colossus prone to crumble under the
first punch and a perfect embodiment of History as
an ineluctable, if perhaps nightmarish, destiny
— a Baal,[16] an Absolute, a secret, a this-worldly

---

[16] In Christian demonology, the principal king of Hell.

mystery stripped of extrahistorical meaning (and the historical meaning of which was equally impenetrable). Victimized by faith, dear Sir, by myth, and not by deeds of one or another Marquis de Sade-like prosecutor in the political apparatus who persecuted the enemies of the system. And because one wasn't at liberty even to try and describe these phenomena in terms drawn from outside the sanctified canon, and because a societal analysis of these phenomena could not even get off the ground, far less get widely disseminated, its unnameability and untouchability only augmented the mystery. My novel is, naturally, not a photograph but a figuration, a model, a metaphor of that reality, just because I don't believe that it is possible to create these very conditions and relations only once; in other words, that all this could never take place under a different sky.

So that, when my protagonist runs into ancient morons in office, potters around secret conference halls, ogles mobilization plans, it is not inconsistency but a demonstration that the extraordinary monolithic character of that faith grew out of indifference — of a very stupid kind.

But perhaps these are experiences that cannot be shared. I'm sitting here and writing a new booklet called *The Mask*.

[...]

****

Cracow, 1 July 1972

[...]

Baloyne is really taken from "life", though obviously not "whole hog"; the abilities represented by this character are rather alien to me (schmoozing and socializing with people for whom I hardly care is for me simply impossible; I don't have any social tactics to fall back on, I simply don't know how to be courteous, platitudinous, attentive, complimentary, even if I wanted to very much, etc.). Aside from that, my typical fears are of "existential", ontological nature rather than psychological, psychoanalytic, or anxiety-related.

[...]

Nihilism? In my books? Perhaps there is something to it, perhaps you are right in some mysterious way. I would call it — futility... that cares to appear not to appear so. To speak awful things with an almost playful innocence, letting go of reins that cannot even be detected... As for Einstein — undoubtedly, he was my youthful idol. And the thought that even monuments of that calibre could do with being pulled down a notch struck me when I was reading Vonnegut's Cat's Cradle — which looked in the beginning like it was going to be a pasquil aimed at this type of a genius, only Vonnegut took a different tack and the whole thing went to the dogs, although maybe he never harboured such intentions in the first place and the whole thing was just in my imagination.

[...]

****

Cracow, 4 July 1972

[...]

Power can be total, yet, in spite of that, remain purely external as a threat. I experienced this in my country during the occupation: you were liable to die on a fleeting whim of any German. Total power not limited to being an external threat is a totally different world. Such power cannot simply present itself as a consequence of brute, naked force. It needs to grandstand in the name of an ideology, e.g., of being a manifestation of a Historical Process. We have had by now a certain amount of elucidation from its proponents of how such ideology is implemented — but none when it comes to its effects on its opponents. Hamlet's assertion, "I could be bounded in a nutshell and count myself a king of infinite space",[17] which implies inner freedom, loses its entire force at this point. We are no longer talking about a particularization of the relation between domination and submission ("father-child", "teacher-students"). Only one story by Kafka, like a lightning bolt, blasted open this whole dimension: "In the Penal Colony". 'Course, I don't need to be reminded who Kafka was and how much we owe him. All the same, in the manner of Hamlet, the characters in The Castle or The Trial remain free inside. Even if only for a while. The officer in the Penal Colony, on the other hand, this calm, non-nonsense technologian of torture, is a prophecy that has come true. This is not to say, of course, that no writer is capable of going beyond Kafka (previously you yourself remarked that I'm trying to go beyond Gombrowicz[18]). Convinced in the end of the futility of his own writings, Kafka demanded that his works be destroyed. His entire legacy gains full depth only in conjunction with this deathbed command (disobeyed by Brod). Libraries have been written on Kafka (in other words, too much...). But what is it that he leads us to in the end? A Mystery. Only this last command — his testament of self-destruction — reveals his defiance at the impenetrability of the Mystery: he spurned it by spurning what he had created. It wasn't a gesture of a coffee-shop scrivener! There is no doubt whatsoever about the futility of going after that Mystery within our order of being (say,

---

[17] Act II, scene 2.
[18] Exiled Polish novelist and dramatist of the absurd (1904–1969).

in Heidegger's sense). Even so, it doesn't follow at
all that there is nothing left to create. Here, I
sense a touchy problem. When my work begins to get
entangled in these considerations, when I ought to
"transcend Kafka", it might look like a declaration
that I "bested Kafka". This is, of course, utter
nonsense. Not because I lack such ambitions, but
because the magnitude of themes a writer attempts
to hoist onto his back IS NOT and can never be a
measure of his success — of his own magnitude.
Our world has different points of reference from
Kafka's; it has opened dimensions beyond those
within which Kafka's protagonists had to soldier on.
This is not to say that the old ones have become
in any way irrelevant: it's just that our hump got
bigger in the meantime. It's not true, in other
words, that there is nothing new under the sun and
that all History is a humdrum repetition of the
past. And even if I am wrong, I'm still right in
pragmatic and psychological terms. Meaning that,
if the psychosocial phenomena that we (and I) had
the ill-fortune to go through had at some other
time been inflicted on others, our culture has no
permanent trace of their experience. The latter
does not exist because too much here just cannot
be interpersonally communicated. Kafka's troubles,
his struggles against his father's will, never
amounted to any kind of provocation — an incursion
of politics into the domain of family relations.
His father was certainly no agent or executive
of destiny as a religious doctrine — as History
itself. In their day these spheres of life were
simply independent of each other. For us, reality
itself fused them together. I don't believe that
any form of power, political system, or domination
is necessarily evil. Looking at this horrible
world, I may feel guilty before my son — but even
if I wanted to follow some kind of orthodoxy in
rearing children, I could never be a Father in
the manner of Kafka's, the uncompromising owner
of Truth, the Determiner of Life Paths. In the old
days such Fathers never doubted their knowledge

and their authority; their paternalism rested on the conviction that they Knew Better than their children what was right. But, at the end of the day, the world of The Castle and the world of The Trial is simply not the world of "In the Penal Colony"...

Though, in a sense, it IS. Is it easier, after all, to die of cancer in your own bed than in a gas chamber with a thousand of other people? Is one even able or allowed to answer questions presented in THIS form? To wit: did reality after Kafka "outdo" the genuinely degenerate era of the Austro-Hungarian empire in which Kafka lived and wrote — by the escalation of evil perpetrated on man by man? One might be forbidden to ask such questions for their brazen arithmetical audacity! But, whereas the amount of pity of which people are at all capable is already a vessel filled to the brim for all places and for all times, there remains a matter of UNDERSTANDING the mechanisms at work — and here I appeal to Pascal and his reed. For I would like to understand and not merely purvey stories that reflect this or that abyss looming before us. To the extent I was entitled to express my views on this subject, I did it in the last chapter of The Philosophy of Chance devoted to an attack on Mann — in which I went after Doctor Faustus with the entire animus I'm capable of, because the Faustian myth to which Mann appealed in his book was none other than an "aggrandizement" of the Nazis' genocidal crime. The evil of the Faustian Satan is "personal" because it is "addressed" at a certain individual; in other words, this individual becomes SELECTED by evil. The whole point, I wrote, is that dying for what one is (or was) belongs to a different order of things than perishing under the aegis of state crime and murder as a nameless human mass — with even names torn off and thrown away. Hence, I concluded, perhaps even without wishing to, but in keeping with a distinguished Mediterranean tradition, Mann beautified and ENNOBLED evil (in its time this polemic had its American version in the debate between Hannah Arendt and Norman Podhoretz concerning the matter of Eichmann — whether he was a "banality" [<u>Eichmann or the Banality of Evil</u>[19]] or, as Podhoretz argued, whether he was in his own way a "negative titan").

Perhaps judgments passed on genocide amount ultimately to the same thing. But the mechanisms of trial and execution are FAR from the same. This is my sole point. Were the gentlemen who slaughtered K. like a hog on the last page of <u>The Trial</u> good family men with pets, flower boxes, and children? In Kafka they are only half-allegorical creations, but when they started living among us, and when in front of our eyes they streamlined their job with the aid of the machinery of murder, they became a problem of a different order... no longer allegorical.

[...]

****

Cracow, 27 July 1972

[...]

I'm writing to touch on two completely different matters. The first is directed at the world, for it occurred to me how to communicate the difference between "universal" and particular evil in political systems. What I was trying to express — even when I couldn't formulate it propositionally, for example, in <u>Memoirs Found in a Bathtub</u> — amounts to the following formula. If a given social system becomes absolutely indistinguishable from its overarching ideology, then it acquires an intentional character. This means that nothing happens therein just because, e.g., out of confusion or somebody's wilfulness or stupidity. Nothing is ever taken as personal or incidental. The system becomes

---

[19] Lem gets the title wrong; it should be *Eichmann in Jerusalem: a Report on the Banality of Evil* (1963).

an embodiment of preestablished harmony, i.e., infallible determinism, so that its absurdities must now be explained in terms of mysterious portents. And this is the point on which I declare war on Orwells of all kinds because their diabolical interpretation elevates the phenomenology of politics — places it on a pedestal of deliberate evil perpetrated for essentially metaphysical motives. Meanwhile, most of the time this evil was quite simply shoddy, lacking any other-worldly sanction — and that's why it is so important that any citizen should always be allowed to scream out his pain, just like any person sitting in a dentist's chair with a drill in his tooth has that right.

[...]

When Klapaucius asks the machine to grant wishes whether it's a Machine to Grant Wishes or a Machine to Ask Questions, you added one word in your translation, so that he asks: "Are you a Machine to Ask Stupid Questions?" It may seem like a monumentally trivial thing; all the same, it is somehow pertinent. I'm hoping that, when you have thought about this minuscule problem, you'll grant that I'm right — that it should read: "Are you a Machine to Ask Questions?" without the modifier "stupid". It's really a matter of sense and sensitivity, of a certain aural aura, for it's rather difficult to argue this point in any other terms. The word that comes to my mind about the way I wrote the story is "**understatement**"; the expression that comes to mind about the way you rendered this passage is "**to overdo it**".[20] With me it's a matter of a certain dryness, matter-of-factness, laconicism, directness, of irony concealed in the subtext; with you this irony is communicated expressis verbis,[21] brought to the surface and spotlighted idiomatically.

---

[20] The translator did make the change (in "A Good Shellacking" in *The Cyberiad*).

[21] Latin: "in express terms".

To be sure, this IS but a detail. But this detail, demarcating the point at which our paths fork, signals perhaps something significant. Namely this: I myself am partly guilty for having strenuously encouraged you not to remain tied to literalness, to let loose the reins, to let style rule supreme. I can see now that I may have been imprudent to do so.

[...]

Perhaps what I'm driving at is that it's important to me that the fantastic be always somehow "grounded", somehow rendered CONCRETE, simply because there's nothing easier than to enter the domain of pure Fantasy where "absolutely everything is possible", whereupon the work loses its genre-given heft, tangibility, weight — its verisimilitude, in a manner of speaking. Here's another example. At one point in the story about King Krool,[22] Trurl and Klapaucius converse on a terrace at dusk. I made the view from the terrace relatively concrete (white houses, darkening sky, etc.), whereas in your version this concreteness was dropped. Naturally, once again this is a mere detail. The point is, however, that the sum total of such details creates the "materiality" of the world presented which ought to endow it with a quasi-realism — so that NOT EVERYTHING in the storyworld should be woven out of inexpressible generalities. The more weird, miraculous, ethereal, and incredible things take place, the more such fantastic elements need to be backed up and "anchored" in SMALL, REALISTIC DETAILS; otherwise you'll end up with something like a "dreamed reality". And the domain of dreams is precisely one I'd like to avoid. I'm not sure, truth be told, if I expressed myself clearly enough???????

[...]

****

[22] "The Second Sally, or the offer of King Krool".

Cracow, 1 August 1972

[...]

In my case, I couldn't make up my mind to have a child for the longest time; together with my wife we were quite opposed to the idea, both for reasons typical of people who think — and of people who suffered the German occupation, since, overall, the world appears to be a very badly constructed place to bring life into, especially given the kind of experiences we both had. Still — there is a time for dying and there is a time for living.

[...]

****

Cracow, 23 August 1972

[...]

I got interested at one point in the theory of machine translation, only to realize the hopelessness of automated procedures. The **sophistication level** — Raffinesse[23] — of a text depends on a variety of factors co-determining the choice of each successive word. In the case of literary works it may be an incalculable set; one that cannot even be ordered in the mathematical sense. Even so, this nature of things does not preclude the formulation of a cogent group of purely practical, utilitarian operating rules. For instance, for Polish and English I imagine the following rule. Compare numerically the size of the Polish and the English texts, making sure first of all that nothing has been lost in translation. On the assumption that nothing or practically nothing has, the English text

[23] German: "refinement".

ought to be shorter than the Polish one since the quantity of bits per letter is statistically greater in English than in Polish. If the English text is longer, it indicates a poor translation. As far as tests go, this one is purely formal, and about as effective as a prayer, but at the same time perhaps not without value.

[...]

You're right to say — in my paraphrase — that it's not ME who should be satisfied with the translation. Naturally! This is a combinatorial structure with three outcomes that, running through all possible states, can assume the following values (K.=Kandel; L.=Lem; P=public opinion; "+" is satisfied and "–" is dissatisfied. K+, L+, P+ (IDEAL STATE). K+, L+, P– (exceptionally idiotic state). K+, L–, P–, and also K+, L–, P+ (peculiar state). K–, L–, P+ (fairly acceptable state). K–, L–, P– (perfectly negative state). No point in considering any others.

[...]

****

Cracow, 4 November 1972

[...]

I'm killing myself trying to write a new book entitled <u>Imaginary Magnitude</u>.[24] I'm really into it, it's an anthology of introductions to nonexistent works, and I concealed within it a preface to my posthumous writings, written from the point of view of a corpse — it's all good fun, but awfully

---

[24] The correct translation should be *Illusions of Grandeur*. Given Lem's acceptance of the canonical version, I'll follow suit, except when demanded by context.

difficult, for you need to be super careful in dosing out this perfidy. It's going to be small, around 100 pages, and more work than Sisyphus had. Still, it'll be quite something, not least since there's a heck of a lot of chutzpah camouflaged in there.

[...]

****

Cracow, 10 November 1972

[...]

Truth is, I've been monstrously delayed and slow in my development, and this can be seen especially on the example of my CYCLES, for instance in Pirx. Not to beat around the bush, the last two stories from the cycle, written during the past few years, aren't bad literature at all, no matter who's judging, whereas all the others that came before are nothing but <u>adroit</u> storytelling in the entertaining mode, nothing more. This is neither a testimony to my success nor to my failure, it's just that I can only create what I'm capable of at any given stage of my artistic development, and there is no denying that this level used to be LOW... I'm glad, at least, that it has risen in the meantime. Thank God for that.

As for the afore-mentioned (i.e., God), in all candour, I'm glad he doesn't exist for, strictly speaking, he would be a being I could not accept — judging by his creation. In any case, this is more or less how I presented it in the recently written voyage of Ijon Tichy — in which robots pursue theodicy. Now I'm churning out other metaphysical pieces and probably for that reason, even though I'm dead on my feet, I'm feeling good. The new book, <u>Imaginary Magnitude</u>, is a Short Anthology of Introductions to Nothing, and should

be interesting even on the visual level. It'll
consist of one introduction after another. First
the Introduction to all Introductions, then the
Introduction to the talks conducted by MIT after
the year 2000 with GOLEM, a kind of electronic guy
with an IQ of about 1600.[25] Then the Introduction to
"The Errant Error" (L'Erreure errante; Der Irrende
Irrtum — a kind of anti-Darwinian conception
of natural evolution approached as involution —
this is more Naturphilosophie than theoretical
biology, according to the opinion of one of my
fictive mavens, for, after all, I only whipped up
the introduction to the Polish edition); then
the Introduction to Extelopedia (by Vestrand
Books — Extrapolative Teleonomic Encyclopedia, or
PRENCYC: prognosticating of Encyclopedia); then
the Introduction to a picture book (by Totentanz
— it's a new form I thought up, X-rays of human
lovemaking, i.e., skeletal porn); finally the
Introductions to three successive editions of my
posthumous works, written from the point of view of
a CORPSE. The whole thing has a rather CADAVEROUS
aura about it and, for that reason, pleases me and
makes me feel rather good. It's a small thing, but
neat.

[...]

Dostoyevsky was a VERY DISAGREEABLE FELLOW — I
think you know something about it. Gombrowicz...
God forbid you had to deal with him on a personal
basis... what an insufferable Superegocentric...
incapable of love, they write nowadays... yep,
that's the way it really was. Well, what you're
gonna do? Writers are to be a panacea for
everything that ails us, even sweep the stairs on
which they tread, and be sweet as sugar as well?
AS FAR AS I'M CONCERNED, Bellow wrote only 2 books:
Henderson the Rain King and Mr. Sammler's Planet

---

[25] It appears to be a typo; later on Lem consistently puts Golem's IQ at 600.

— both excellent and both bloody far-flung from one another — you can tell the writer's class by his <u>range</u>. On the other hand, types who pander to the public sicken me even if they are all marzipan character-wise.

You haven't read Faulkner? You'll have a laugh since, besides <u>Sartoris</u> and <u>Absalom, Absalom!</u>, which I wolfed greedily, I practically haven't read anything else. In a sense, if you know one Faulkner novel, you know them all. When the chips are down, I'm just a normal monster so that the stuff that interests Faulkner leaves me completely cold; if it was up to me, I'd let loose the health service, ethnologists, social workers, and of course <u>police</u> and other administrative departments onto his territory (Yoknapatawpha). Here comes Lem the moralist-meliorist... With Dostoyevsky it was a different story, because he was an altogether ordinary genius, meaning, when he wanted to write trash, nothing doing, a real King Midas, whatever he touched turned into gold, he could transform a visit to an old whore into metaphysics of the highest order ("Apropos of the Wet Snow"[26]) — on the other hand, when he slipped, as OCCASIONALLY he did, then he wiped out WHOLEHOG, snout first. Oh, he was the biggest matrioshka of all, one of those Russian dolls that contains all the smaller ones inside. You couldn't transcend him if you tried. You always get stuck in the end.

[...]

PS. **Yes: I am really THAT strong — and TRULY is NON SERVIAM my device.**[27]
PPS. Except for my parents, the Germans slaughtered my entire family (mainly gas — death camps). **And so I think it is our DUTY to read Borowski.** I never drove over to see the Auschwitz museum and don't

---

[26] Part II of *Notes From the Underground*; the prostitute, Liza, is actually young.
[27] By "device", Lem means "motto".

intend to — **I know it all firsthandedly.** But Borowski — **well, that is a must.**[28]

[...]

****

Cracow, 19 November 1972

[...]

Meanwhile I'm hammering away at the typewriter, writing the most horrible, i.e., the most audacious (not in the artistic sense — bugger that) things that are only possible to conceive in this life, retrofitting it into <u>Imaginary Magnitude</u>. Since I'm putting these words — they're about our species — into the iron mouth of a computer perched at the top of the highest Tower of Babel of intelligence, I don't need to lose sleep over it — 'course, I could never get away with it myself, but there's no stopping that guy... Still, it's drudgery like hell since, after all, I've got to simulate an IQ of 600. Exactly 600 — not an iota less.

[...]

PS. My agent is trying to elbow one of my fairy tales about the erotic life of robots into the German-language edition of <u>Playboy</u>. **The climax of my career is approaching, the time of my life** when I appear in <u>Playboy</u>. Ha! Who'd ever have believed it?

[...]

****

---

[28] Tadeusz Borowski, *This Way for the Gas, Ladies and Gentlemen* (1947).

Cracow, 7 December 1972

[...]

A while back, it seems, I wrote something foolish, even though, it goes without saying, you had seduced me into that folly (I'm speaking of "non serviam" as my motto). It isn't, because my atheism is cold, chilled — neither overly despairing nor excessively angry (although you did write something funny about the way in which I supposedly banished God from my intellect for Bad Behaviour)... No, seriously speaking, this is not at all so. But, ultimately — we are talking about LITERATURE, which is to say that the game does not take place in our own intellectual backyard but, rather, in between massive CULTURAL MIRRORS; meaning that, if billions of human beings (not too dissimilar from me) believed, believe, and will believe in God, I cannot but accept that faith as a reference point in my writings. On the other hand, more than once I carried out a reductio ad absurdum of faith, of God, still other times of the VESTED INTEREST on which such faith feeds. So what that death will look into your eyes and mine, that one day a gaping black hole will yawn before us — Non Serviam means: thou shalt not — I shall not — delude myself out of servile fear. (NB., you've read His Master's Voice, haven't you? What happened in there to Dr Rappaport is what happened to me. In 1941, when the German troops marched into Lvov, I was going to be shot dead — barring one extra element, the call for a volunteer, everything described in the book is true... I tried at that moment, by appealing to a fiction of ad hoc reincarnation, simply to help myself get through the final few moments, to keep a stiff upper lip, as they say, right up to the moment of death. God's help, you see, was such a blatant lie to me that there never was any question of even trying to appeal to it...) **so I was already tested.** Hence Non serviam — and nothing else.

[...]

Just now, writing Golem's **big speech** about Man, I went through 500 sheets of paper — the room turned white since I'm in the habit of tossing rejects on the floor — to end up with 30 pages. I couldn't find the right TONE, quite apart from winching myself up to the IQ level of 600... at last I'm starting to hear a certain Grandeur, as if the words were, indeed, coming from Above. We'll see — maybe it'll work. <u>Imaginary Magnitude</u> is about NOT writing the books about which it speaks in the Introductions rather than about writing them — Love, Longing, Hope, Greatness, Happiness: all of them feed on NOT COMING ABOUT. So my writing precipitates around this aspect of not coming about.

[...]

Well. Am I a popular writer? Yes, but only thanks to my WORSE books, the earlier ones! I've been working on a **hill-climbing gradient** not because it was my cunning plan, but because I was very slow in my mental development — my readers, poor souls, accompanied me on that voyage, for what else were they to do? Really, I keep getting so many entreaties in letters — to GIVE UP... to be more simple... to write like in <u>The Invincible</u>... or at least like in <u>Solaris</u>... And me: No and No — again, not out of pride or because I consciously made such a decision, but only because I am like a bird: I sing the only way I know how, and the way I used to sing yesterday is no longer in me today!

Having said that, generally speaking I owe the label **"popular writer"** (mind you, I'm not knocking it, just **investigating** it: I much prefer to look into things rather than just label them) to what is more readable among my works than to what is better. Ok, ok, I'll take home the Nobel Prize, if you so insist! We'll split it — do you like driving very big cars? Cadillac Eldorado, or something like that... eh, c'mon, here it flows in, there it runs out, aqua destilata[29]...

[...]

****

Cracow, 1 February 1972

[...]

GOLEM'S LECTURE which, I trust, you have received by now together with my previous letter, has in the meantime gone through some changes. I wrote the first 8-10 pages anew and differently since the old version wasn't as brainy and lucid as I wished, although the overall voice did not change in the end. The other book (Imaginary Magnitude) finally went into production.

Mrs. Ready[30] is currently midwifing my first American children, Memoirs Found in a Bathtub and The Invincible, into the world. Having to write an afterword to a new edition of Wells's War of the Worlds, I read it again after some 30 years and found it superb, perhaps the best thing that ever came out of this English Colossus. Seems no one will ever be able to write LIKE THAT again, in accordance with Heraclitus's dictum that you can't step twice into the same river.

[...]

****

---

[29] Latin: "distilled water"; Lem's self-deprecating distich rhymes in Polish.
[30] Lem's then American editor.

Cracow, 28 February 1973

[...]

Today I'm starting once weekly lectures at the Jagiellonian University — on the face of it on SF, but really "de omnis rebus et quibusdam aliis"[31] — the fashion of extending invitations to writers, also writers of SF, came to our universities I don't know when or how. The student body: youthful, long-haired, unwashed, likeable, but, I sense, generally undereducated — these young people DON'T FEEL LIKE doing almost ANYTHING at all. It's sad, really...

[...]

****

Cracow, 11 April 1973

[...]

Both the title (ILLUSIONS of grandeur) as well as sundry remarks made in passing in the text are meant to amplify the illusion of genius and even more so of the superhumanity of the speaker. Most of all, the three texts preceding the Lecture, namely the "civilian" introduction by someone from MIT, the "God Bless America" introduction penned by some retired general (**US Army, ´ret.**), plus the instructions for people who participate in talks with Golem for the first time — allow one to question the unequivocal assertiveness of Golem's speeches. Indeed, all these factors — as well as the fragments of Extelopedia — rob his lecture of full assertion. The hope offered to listeners during the last stages of the address is thus of DUBIOUS

---

[31] Latin: "about everything and other things besides".

nature, meaning it's shot through with irony — but you guessed it, and all the praise to you for that. Implicitly, Golem suggests that Humanity will become more and more LIKE HIM, if we are to become his equal in intelligence; still, I guess, you cannot approach the plan of "supercomputerization" of Homo without irony, without derision, since we're talking about a freedom to redesign ourselves condemned from the start by contradictions (what kind of freedom is it when we are nudged toward it by the technocivilizational gradient?). Hence the rhetoric of the pompous ending would be undercut if — which cannot be excluded — I were ever to say something again through those metal lips. Golem is, no doubt, an egocentric. The crucial point, not made salient in the lecture itself, is the question of the credibility of THIS kind of address — when the speaker indisputably towers over the listeners, you can hardly separate description (the independent state of the designated phenomenon) from normative prognosis. Not everything in there is sacred truth believed by the speaker himself...

Personification is a rhetorical ploy, at least prima facie — I've got the theodicy according to Golem sketched in notebooks; perhaps I'll return to it sometime. Anyway, personification is the outcome of a recurrent projection (speaking of Nature's or Evolution's technology, one involuntarily assumes teleonomic causality, at least in a fraction of what such "technology" denotes). Not to dance around the issue, Golem is not the final stage of development (he speaks of standing "a little higher" than humanity on the intellectual ladder), and there is no reason why he could not go on expanding. However, all such approximations of the Absolute (omniscience) are doomed to failure which is all the more apparent for being successful at each successive stage (since, at the end of the day, God cannot be engineered technologically, and each step, i.e., each amplification of intelligence, must bring one closer to the end of the road just because the world certainly does not allow constructing intellects of arbitrary magnitude — so that, the higher any such intellect is able to hoist itself, the more acutely it must realize that the game is ultimately doomed to failure and that the magnitude of failure is directly proportional to the magnitude of unfulfilled hope).

[...]

Progress and Golem. Well, even if the concept IS to some extent undermined by camouflaged derision, one shouldn't assume that Golem first knocks down the concept of progress only to restore it later. The bottom line is that he's a kind of "it" from a game of "Simon says" we used to play in childhood, lecturing "Simon says do as I do!" Or maybe he doesn't even wholly grasp the HORRENDOUS character of his postulates...

SFWA[32] has just offered me a choice of memberships, honorary or regular, a delicate matter since, when all is said and done, they are a club of morons...

[...]

****

Cracow, 17 July 1973

[...]

We're in the grip of a terrible heat wave and, what without air-conditioning, I can't write. I fear that air-conditioning may also become at a premium in the States. If we were still in the era of kingdoms, futurologists would be the first to lose their heads on the block.

[...]

[32] Science Fiction Writers of America.

"**Juvenile**" has two aspects: **immaturity** and childishness, and they are not the same. I think that there is something childish in the conception of science itself, first of all as faith in the assumption that the world is comprehensible at all and, second, as an emotional attachment to the current state of knowledge which, in the light of all information supplied by the history of science, is always transient. This type of faith is typical of children. SF, on the other hand, is, I have to say, first and foremost immature. Eternally immature.

My wife and I read your sketch of Lem's spiritual profile with the greatest interest. It's true that I'm not vain: knowledge and intellect preclude vanity by being **self-reflexive**, by being reminders of the paltriness and ephemerality of one's achievements. **Vanity of Ideas** — you got that right surprisingly well! Really.

America's future... dark, most likely, but should it turn completely into a police state, it will be a different one from those familiar to us from European history; history doesn't waste time on primitive autoplagiarism. It's not even that Nixon is such a crook, but that he is so inept in hiding the fact that he is a crook. In a president of the U.S. ineptness is a fatal character flaw.

In the story about the Pirate Pugg[33] I made a simple mistake about the number of electrons! I'd be much obliged for a correction since later on critics spin the wildest hypotheses from such lapses...

[...]

****

---

[33] "The Sixth Sally" from *The Cyberiad*.

Cracow, 8 August 1973

[...]

Writing always comes to me with the greatest effort and you can gauge what I've accomplished by the animal pig-headedness of my renewed struggles. In this I'm a total beast of burden — like ants that will always go about rebuilding their hill from scratch in the same way even if you destroy it a hundred times. That's why, if I sometimes run out of strength, i.e., stamina, the final text may end up being not as polished as it should. Probably this is why Summa technologiae is more lucid and accessible than The Philosophy of Chance, to which, I repeat, I lack the strength to return, even though I ought to. If so, however, it wouldn't be a matter of revision; I'd have to demolish everything and start over. I'm afraid I have no patience for that.

Mrs. Ursula Le Guin wrote to me that her nine-year-old son, to whom she read two fragments from The Cyberiad (I don't know which ones) in your translation, became quite worked up that there weren't more.

[...]

****

Cracow, 30 August 1973

[...]

At the moment I'm reading (in French) Hannah Arendt's The Origins of Totalitarianism. I didn't know this book before, I was familiar only with her Eichmann in Jerusalem. A very intelligent broad. I assume you read her books? Strange impression after reading! No question, she diabolized both forms of totalitarianism, since, 1) she endowed them with pure existential autonomy "<u>per genus proximum et differentiam specificam</u>", and 2) she attributed to them full intentionality. Of course, her distinction between tyranny, absolutism, and dictatorship on one hand and totalitarianism on the other is dogmatic in the sense that, as a dichotomy, it plays up the differences where in reality the changes were <u>continuous</u>, incremental, minute, gradual, and this is only point 1; point 2 is that she made out these systems to be the fruit of <u>strictly</u> intentional evil, i.e., a result of actions fully cognizant of their social anti-rationality — all this in order to obtain a "pure distillate" of something that was never there in the first place, of sociopolitical formations devoid of even a hint of utilitarianism or pragmatism; this is to say that, in either case, apart from the Axis of Evil (such as Hitler), "there was nobody" (according to her) who might have <u>gained</u> from it in the sense of "<u>id fecit cui prodest</u>".[34] For these reasons, but also because of her quasi-Talmudic tendency to abstraction, to conducting her investigative labours on already formulated abstractions of the first order, her book is at once fascinating and insufficiently precise in terms of "<u>adaequatio rei et intellectus</u>".[35] It is an essay in (partly) fantastic sociology — or, in short, Science Fiction... And yet, by the <u>very</u> exaggeration, simplification, and violence inflicted on factual material in order to tailor it to her a priori conception, she succeeded in recreating a certain "aura", a certain "<u>genius temporis acti</u>"[36] of times which I know like the back of my hand from personal acquaintance. It is interesting that <u>hyperbolization</u>, <u>emphasis</u>, macabre, "black oratory" — in one word, the <u>Ersatz</u> of infernal transcendence — are the very means by which one can evoke social and factual states that the painstaking sensibility of ordinary sociological analyses can't crack. Then

---

[34] Latin: "he did it who benefits from it".
[35] Latin: "adequacy of the intellect to the thing (to be known)".
[36] Latin: "essence of time past".

again, maybe it's not so strange after all, since we're talking here about a procedure typical to literature: aiming at "higher", global, visionary truth by way of rungs and steps that <u>are not</u> literal equivalents of factual truth.

[...]

****

Cracow, 4 October 1973

[...]

I must, nonetheless, contend — in keeping with what I believe, and bolstered by the authority of Gombrowicz, whom I hold in very high esteem — that what may be TRUE in terms of the identification and explicit articulation of real (realistic) signifiers of a literary work may be, at the same time, beside the point. Such irrelevance is demonstrated by a simple thought experiment whereby you read two books about exactly the same things, exactly the same relations between people and ideology, of which one is utterly worthless in artistic terms. It follows that the determination of the "final" TRUTH — in other words, the plumbing of the propositional "rock bottom" of the work (though it may constitute the inalienable right and even the obligation of the critic) — isn't the same as determining its uniqueness, its value, its originality. It tells us nothing about whether, in accordance with its poetics, the work succeeded in creating an autonomous storyworld or whether, at the end of the day, the meaning that the critic dug out and identified in its ROOT form is draped in linguistic cloth that is deadly tiresome, opaque, and tedious. In Gombrowicz's case, when overzealous critics tried to "fix" his works "once and for all" by supposedly CORRECTLY IDENTIFYING what is buried

at their semantic BOTTOM — which is to say, by
going "all the way down" in order to tell it like
it is — vehemently and rightly Gombrowicz always
took exception to such moves. After all, literature
draws its power not from what played the role of
a pebble that irritated the artist's soul, like a
grain of sand that irritates the sensitive tissue of
pearl-bearing molluscs, but from the finished PEARL
brought into being by this process — and you cannot
fully explain the PEARL by slicing it open to show
us the pebble that brought it into existence. The
irritant lies behind it, not a shadow of a doubt
about it, but this type of diagnosis neither
exhausts the matter of the pearl's "immanence" nor
hands us the key to understanding why the pearl
is so pleasing. I realize that this old metaphor
is awfully trite but it suits me here. Literature
is being itself — literature is at its best — when
the games it plays occupy a place between a total
linguistic free-for-all, between a celebration of
irresponsibility and the domain of the fundamental,
burdensome, realistic, gloomy, and most of the time
repulsive truths, facts, and things that make up
existence.

[...]

****

Cracow, 26 November 1973

[...]

Perhaps the main point is that the world today
has shrunk to one completely interconnected whole.
Friends and (alleged) enemies of the OPEC countries
experience very similar problems, irrespective
of whether they were the intended target or not.
Moreover, current articles in Newsweek, Time,
International Herald Tribune, Le Monde are all in

the key of "Doomsday". As if what <u>The Limits of Growth</u> place only in the 21st century has ALREADY begun.

In spite of the circumstances — assuming it's true that the world is menaced by global recession, assuming that not only gas but eggs and paper will be (or are) in scarce supply, that book publication becomes beset by difficulties... in spite of these circumstances, I'm not contemplating re-training myself for a more immediately useful profession.

[...]

I've been ill a little, worked a little (though not too much), seen a few of my books come out here and there, but at the moment my principal pastime, although not an especially happy one, is poring over all the above-mentioned periodicals. Anyway, I'm coming to the conclusion that Nixon is truly an exceptional scoundrel, not to mention a totally unparalleled liar, so that now, in addition to all the other problems in the world, America has to deal with the nasty matter of **"impeachment"** — for, in my opinion, even if it were eventually to come to nothing, this one problem will fester and menace the country for a long time yet.

[...]

****

Cracow, 1 December 1973

[...]

We are far from living on different planets; since 1 December, i.e., as of today, we have a countrywide speed limit of 80 km (50 miles) an hour. The Arabs, as it is widely understood by now, have only exposed the latent crisis that characterizes the global energy system. Perhaps one day we will, indeed, need to convey to them our gratitude insofar as the prophecy from The Limits of Growth, hereby confirmed experimentally, so to say, may yet educate and influence the thinking of politicians and economists (deep down I can't say I really believe so).

I'm continuously reading the foreign press (International Herald Tribune, Newsweek or Time, Süddeutsche Zeitung, Journal de Genève) to keep myself up to date. And a couple of days ago I gave a lecture at the Cardinal's Palace in Cracow in front of His Eminence and the assembled clergy on the state of our civilization... I spoke, needless to say, about the energy crisis and had the rather dismal pleasure of citing what I had prophesied on the subject of energy and our civilization already in the first edition (1964) of Summa technologiae. I would rather have been wrong...

No one knows the real consequences, be they economic or a fortiori socio-cultural, of what is currently beginning to happen; personally, I think that events will take a different course from what is imagined by various experts. The role of futurologists in all this is a sad farce. I tried to find anything at all about what we're going through in the countless volumes of prognoses for the years 1975-1985, but much of the time the word ENERGY does not even appear in any of the indices... Matter of fact, I'm thinking to myself, I'd better exercise CAUTION in my works of science fiction. First, as soon as I published The Futurological Congress in the December 1970 issue of Szpilki[37] (the novel begins with street riots), the same things took place in our streets; now that I published a story about civilizational collapse in the same magazine, a week later we were hit with the petrochemical crisis... These are STRANGE OMENS, dear Sir, on top of the fact that Comet Kohoutek is approaching. Although I'm not at all superstitious, all these coincidences seem to be rather curious.

[37] (Polish) *Pins*: satirical weekly.

[...]

I can understand the difficult position in which America finds itself — I would dub the shock "the Titanic effect". By analogy with the passengers of that massive transatlantic liner who could not get it into their heads that their magnificent colossus might be sunk by a collision with an iceberg, the people who witnessed Americans walk on the Moon can't wrap their heads around the fact that this achievement does not secure in the least the longterm health of their social life. The surprise that everything can come crashing down SO EASILY dominates the articles I've been reading, not even so much as a conscious realization but rather as a psychological reflex, not fully grasped by the columnists.

[...]

In any case, I'm 95 percent certain that if ½ of the expenditures that go into armaments (the Arab-Israeli war cost about 14 billion dollars) had been diverted to **Research and Development** into energy and "civilizational homeostasis", we would be reaping the harvest right now, instead of relying on **"crash programs"** that are being mounted as I speak (N.B., **Nixon is of course a crook, and a big one,** and Truman was right to call him **a damned liar** — it is by now crystal clear that he is nothing but a pathological liar, a shyster, a man with ZERO class, a PETTY thug — and this is a disaster.)

Let's not exaggerate our so-called growing prosperity; I assure you that even if the standard of living in the U.S. dropped 300 or 400 percent, it would still remain extraordinary in comparison to the wasteful grind of our march in place.

[...]

****

Cracow, 24 January 1974

[...]

It so happens that, happily (to the extent one can put it that way), I almost died twice. The first time was by now long ago, when I was to be exterminated like a cockroach during the German occupation; the second time was around 1960. That second incident was more protracted. I was suffering then from symptoms that, according to our best medical knowledge, are indicative of coronary thrombosis (<u>angina pectoris</u>) — acute and persistent pain radiating into the arm and the shoulder blade, aching skin around the heart region and on my back, both killing me alive since neither would abate no matter what the doctors did (no one could ever count the pills I chewed through — I used to swallow nitroglycerine tablets like penny candy, to no avail). The pain would recede only when I was unconscious, i.e., when I was asleep, and I was able to sleep only after ingesting powerful cocktails of various drugs. I went to all the top cardiologists, I lost count of the times I had the EKG, sometimes the pain convulsed me when I was behind the wheel, at times so brutally I wasn't sure I'd make it to the nearest pharmacy. At first, my work was a total ruin, among other reasons because the drugs I was on (including tranquilizers like bromide and barbiturates) made me woozy as hell. I was 39 and convinced that I could last maybe a year or two, four at the outside, but without being able to work. I can say without hyperbole that I ate through a whole pharmacy then; I tried everything the doctors recommended and everything they didn't (for example, alcohol). Plus I read everything ever written on the subject. In our country there is a fundamental rule that you don't tell patients the terminal news — this tradition of noble deception is deeply rooted. Still, I knew that nobody had any doubts whatsoever that it was the coronary. In the end, it went away by itself after 2.5 years. (I have my own theory on this subject, I realize you're not a specialist, so I'll say it in two words: there must have been something going on in my shoulder plexus (<u>plexus brachialis</u>) that produced symptoms typical of damaged myocardial vessels; that something resulted in a slight incapacity of the fingers of my left hand — caused by this unknown damage to the motor nerves — but then it receded, i.e., burned itself out, so that all that was left was this incapacity as well as a slow atrophy of my thener and hypothener muscle groups in the left arm.) Now, for the psychological damage. I died a number of times, i.e., I anticipated what was in store for me, and in the end the only consolation I found was work. You couldn't identify this period from my bibliography, i.e., from the chronology of my publications, since after a few months of torturing myself I decided to keep on writing — and I did. (NB., I went on writing even when I had shingles, and this is one of the most excruciatingly painful — although not the most dangerous — afflictions known to medicine. I had to write half-naked since I couldn't bear even the touch of the shirt on my chest; but that's another story). Naturally, I was terrified, but only periodically — curiously, there were periods during which I regarded death with total indifference and others when I was overwhelmed by panic (or panic plus rage, chiefly because it was interfering with the time I had left). Work saved me psychologically, no doubt, even though it had no effect on the pain itself. All the same, during that time I was very hard on the people close to me — I reckon I was very difficult to live with since, alas, the art of dissimulating, of acting out some kind of role, is not within my power. The fact that I used to torment my wife (by not concealing my depression — which I cannot do; I can cover up physical pain but not its psychological correlative) makes me feel disconsolate to this day whenever I think about it. I was able to shield myself with fatalism for a few hours, for a day, but not for months. At the end of the day, losing myself in work was a life saver.

[...]

PS. Of the three cardiologists who treated me for longer periods, two are already dead.

[...]

****

Cracow, 6 March 1974

[...]

The Cyberiad[38] doesn't look bad at all, and Mróz's drawings came out even better than in the Polish original. The book is to be released officially on April 15th, while in the meantime they are supposed to be "promoting" it. Maybe if in the meantime I hijacked a plane, raped all the stewardesses, and dined on the pilot's leg, it would be good for **"promotion"**. But I'm too old for that, and just can't be bothered.

[...]

****

Cracow, 30 March 1974

[...]

Removing narrative "obstacles" cannot be the primary directive of creativity for the same reason

---

[38] Lem is referring to a pre-publication copy of the first English edition.

that the opinion that one could "facilitate" the pleasures of mountain climbing by sawing off the entire base of Mount Everest and dumping the SUMMIT in the middle of a flat lowland — so that everyone could leave his footprint at the top without breaking a sweat — is patent nonsense. The <u>difficulty</u> of the climb is, after all, the <u>integral element</u> of the whole process. Were it any different, you could obtain the same degree of satisfaction from climbing to the same altitude in a helicopter. The reader who refuses his active cooperation is not even so much a child that doesn't like spinach and carrots but one that demands a meal that has already been PRECHEWED. The trend towards "impeding the process of reading", characteristic of contemporary literature, isn't after all an invention of a few empty-headed blokes. Naturally, if these impediments lead absolutely NOWHERE, they become just a blind alley. <u>The Futurological Congress</u> is a kind of parable of consumerist society — society progressing towards total COMFORT as a PRIMARY DIRECTIVE of existence — and these attitudes precipitate the collapse of authentic values, the very ones that arose in the course of history. In contradistinction, "psychem" represents the ultimate and universal technology of the said comfort. The conclusion implies, however, the possibility that the world runs on a different principle, that there is a point at which instrumental hedonism is forced to PAY UP for its excesses, and the payment turns out to be pretty nightmarish. (At least IT'S POSSIBLE to interpret the book in this way, although there are other ways too). As usual in literature, the translation of "what the author wanted to say" into propositional form reveals, at the end of the day, that the whole story was rather banal. (Dostoyevsky's message in <u>Notes from the Underground</u> is also altogether banal — namely, that the "crystal palace" of civilizational well-being cannot be the authentic goal of our strivings, that it's a goal ILL-CONCEIVED, and that Man — in the person of the narrator — will resist it even if it means retreating into madness and meanness, for, as an idiot or a maniac, he is somehow truthful to the core of his humanity — which can be made "angelic" only in the minds of extremely retarded instrumental utopians.) At least, such an interpretation of Dostoyevsky is EMINENTLY admissible.

[...]

It is clear that one shouldn't wait with bated breath for my titles to start climbing up bestseller lists in the U.S. To figure out how to manufacture a bestseller is easy enough, e.g., by reading The Exorcist — everyone understands what it means when a girl possessed by the devil masturbates with a crucifix. It's not difficult to churn out such stuff if you recognize the ingredients that add up to the genius tempori (today: irrationalism blowing the veneer of rationalism out of the water, two-bit demonism, a seagull that shuttles back and forth between the Great Gull in the Sky, and other such twaddle — just because the march of the instrumentally accelerating civilization is perceived as a menacing coercion, so that solutions are sought not in rational analyses of the nature of things but in escapism for which any prettily painted door or any evasion will do — in SF Robert Silverberg is up to the same tricks). Personally I prefer writers who feed such pap to the public CYNICALLY, realizing that they truck in false values and ersatz substrates, to guys like Blatty and Silverberg who have deluded themselves into believing in the authentic value of what they purvey — just because the former haven't yet forfeited a better knowledge of human existence, while the latter, after first wilfully blinding themselves, are only pulling wool over empty eye-sockets. **Streaking** is another chip off the same block, and so is the fashion for "naturalness" (let the body stink, don't wash, don't cut hair, don't shave, go about in rags in search of "human authenticity", precisely where this authenticity is altogether inessential and meaningless).

[...]

****

Cracow, 5 April 1974

[...]

As a prolegomenon towards the sociology of literature or maybe biographical studies: the way I look at it, (literary) talent is not unlike physical ability. To extend the analogy, both can be employed and exploited in various ways. In a way, if somebody is endowed with talent, it's a little like being endowed with immunity to infectious diseases: you don't know in advance which microbes you can take on and which ones you'd better avoid. Things are no different when it comes to writers. Nobody knows in advance which area of literature he is best suited for, in terms of optimal fitness. You have to discover it as you go. I think I was avid about science before I became avid about writing, and the fact that at first I kept these two domains separate inside me, unaware that they could be cross-pollinated, proved detrimental to my fledgling efforts. On the other hand, I've always been gifted when it came to imitating all manner of styles. For example, having read a few books on neopositivism, some time around 1946 I wrote a treatise that was stylistically indistinguishable from your "standard neopositivistic monograph". But a lot of water had to pass under the bridge before my scientific studies permeated my non-scientific writings. Today we employ the term "paradigm" to describe what used to go by the name of "spirit" of disciplinary research. "Spirit" got replaced, then, by a structure or, to put it in colloquial terms, by a skeleton. The scientific skeleton can be detected in any number of my works — of course, we're talking here about influences that manifest themselves paradigmatically and not in any literal sense, e.g., in terms of a theme. Furthermore, this skeleton of mine is hybridized. Take The Cyberiad — isn't it fables from One Thousand and One Nights crossed with the subset of a general systems theory that deals with theoretical studies of bio-logic? "How the World Was Saved"[39] is nothing else than a story rooted in applied logic (semantic rather than pragmatic). "Dragons of Probability" is a theory of probability run through physics run through belles lettres. And so on. Naturally, there aren't that many readers of literature capable of drawing pleasure from decoding both spheres of influence that fuse in these HYBRIDS. Consequently, for a great number of years I was regarded in Poland as an author of popular stories for young readers — and there is no lack of voices who say so to this day. Then there is another factor, namely that the set of readers familiar with my publications in, for example, Philosophical Studies, is hardly coterminous with the set of readers familiar with The Cyberiad (at the very least one must allow for such a possibility). Not much has changed in the meantime, either, if you consider that the Polish press has recently published a smattering of minute reviews of Imaginary Magnitude which peg it as a collection of satirical pastiches of learned Introductions. Judging by this reception, the possibility that I had not written a book of sendups didn't even enter the reviewers' minds. I can't deny, though, that my perfidy lies in writing serious stuff while pretending that it's all a jest. Jesting is my "certificate of insanity", my free-admission pass. But where traditionally this type of writing was recognized only in the form

---

[39] Opening story in *The Cyberiad*; "Dragons of Probability" is the Third Sally.

of "political-philosophical allusions", I've been trying to expand its scope.

[...]

In his comments on novel writing, Forster (Passage to India) flayed Ulysses, calling it an attempt to smear the entire universe with mud. Literary scholars today regard this passage as Forster's disastrous mistake. I don't think so. Ulysses is the fruit of incredible linguistic and imitative dexterity (marvellous language and a magnificent ability to change the narrative poetics in each of the 16 chapters). But, outside the formidable linguistic finesse of the camera eye, what's the point of all this? Merely that Joyce had it in for his Catholic upbringing and decided to show what it was like, warts and all. But what do we find out about Dedalus from Ulysses? Practically nothing, compared to Bloom. At the end of the day, Bloom's erotomania turns out to be a hundred times more important than the continuation of the "portrait of an artist as a young man". What artist are we talking about here? Myself, I've never been perturbed by this book. If your soul is equipped with its own private little inferno, like mine is, you can only laugh at such painted devils. Still, for me Ulysses has always been a watershed, a turning point in the history of modern writing — a turn towards linguistic window-dressing, as I call it. Beautiful prose is everything, without a hint of the abyss. The only abyss the book points to is situated between phalluses and the orifices into which they can be inserted. This is not the same abyss that Dostoyevsky had in mind, and not located in the same place either. Hence this historical fork in the road. What I'm trying to say, in practical terms, is that a writer must beware of running the plough of his verbal prowess over fallow ground. If you've got nothing to show besides linguistic acrobatics, better sit still. This, in essence, is my entire credo. It has a bearing, I think, on the issue of the **prospective saleability** of my books. I started out as an author for young adults and it took umpteen years before somebody noticed that I no longer quite fitted this label. Furthermore, by the very nature of things I appeared on the Polish market in the order of my progressive maturation as a writer. First there were the simpler parts of The Star Diaries, then came **some sophistication**. First Robotic Fables,[40] then The Cyberiad. First A Perfect Vacuum, then Imaginary Magnitude. AND SO FAR I REMAIN THE ONLY PERSON TO NOTICE IT; no Polish critic has wised up to it yet. (Solaris was the climactic point on another, parallel road). But the conception of Man as a being created by stochastic processes, or the search for God as a manoeuvre in search of deliverance — not in terms of the continuation of the soul but in terms of saving this element of evolutionary processes from being discredited in terms of what they produced — all this (these are only two examples, I'm not going to enumerate others) comes directly from Darwin interpreted in the spirit of the 20th-century technological revolution. I've been always trying to integrate everything that could be integrated, and in this sense I've always been completely serious in my work, and whoever is incapable of perceiving it is bound to find it boring, contrived, **"heavy-handed"**, as Silverberg wrote about The Cyberiad, and other such. Contemporary, canonical forms of writing do not, after all, allow belletrists to exercise their right to think...

In this sense I'm completely anachronistic and completely modernistic, which is to say that I come a bit from the 19th century, a bit from the 21st, but the least from the 20th. At least that's how I see it — and all this should have a clear bearing on the reception of my books, rendering them poor candidates for bestsellers. Is this bad? I confess, if I could write bestsellers according to the formulas of today, I wouldn't bother (unless

---

[40] Much of it translated as *Mortal Engines*.

I were somebody else, in which case all speculation becomes utterly meaningless).

[...]

****

Zakopane, 10 June 1974

[...]

It's pouring like hell, dumping snow in the mountains, and I'm sitting here and writing The Mask.[41] Earlier on I finished Golem's second lecture ("About Itself", i.e., Golem on Golem) as well as "Confession",[42] quite a strange story about a hunting machine that relates, by means of internal monologue, how she sallied forth into the world in pursuit of her Victim, only later to come to the conclusion that maybe it was unnecessary to kill him, so that she continued to track him but only in order to shower him with caresses. (At first she was a wondrously ravishing woman who had no inkling that she was an apparatus programmed to kill the guy, but when love entered the picture, filled with misgivings she sliced her belly open and could see dormant in her body a large silver larva which, having then crawled out of its cocoon, hastened anew in the tracks of the Lover. The narration changes the grammatical form at this point from neuter to female: first "it walked", "it travelled", but later "she walked", "she ran", which cannot really be accurately rendered in any non-Slavic language.) To me it's the negative of Solaris — Rheya (or Harey, if you will) placed this time around in a slightly

---

[41] A 1976 collection including the eponymous novelette, originally published in 1974 in the magazine *Kultura*; in English "The Mask" appeared in *Mortal Engines*.

[42] Judging by the content, the working title of "The Mask".

different situation and speaking from introspection. Quite an eerie, lyrical, ghastly, melancholy, and — as my wife tells me — psychologically Feminine piece. Ha! Am I not a stranger even to myself?

[...]

****

Cracow, 10 July 1974

[...]

It's relatively easy to make a great majority of average (normal) people inflict suffering on others; this is exhibited, among other things, by the experiments conducted a year ago or so by American psychologists (alas, I can't remember their names or the locations of these experiments; I read about them in some scientific journal).[43] These facts of the matter don't square with the popular assumption of a certain decency in human nature — although human nature is, in reality, neither decent nor "indecent", but only extremely pliable in various contexts. Interesting questions arise, in truth, only when the said torments and agonies are inflicted as flat-out deliverance, i.e., when they are paraded as a "virtuous protectorate", or as love of fellow human beings, in the very situations when the values that are allegedly being protected are, in fact, being destroyed. The mechanisms enabling such actions prove to be surprisingly simple, commonly relying on turning inside out the context in which evil is perpetrated by solemnly rechristening it as glorious good. Even as the oppressed are labelled

---

[43] Lem may be thinking of Stanley Milgram's 1961 experiments, first described in 1963 in the *Journal of Abnormal and Social Psychology* and in greater depth in his 1974 book, *Obedience to Authority: An Experimental View.*

"subhuman" or "non-human", their liquidation can be maintained to be necessitated by the "general good" of the future generations, etc.; or that humanity must be erased from the face of the earth in the name of humanity — this last point of view is not as deranged as it might appear, insofar as it forms the basis of the lion's share of contemporary military-strategic doctrines. Factors that hinder such actions are also simple in nature. The idea that with the help of a company of commandos one can "remove" the royal family or the government in order to impose a "better government" can creep into the mind of both an English or a Congolese general, but whereas the Englishman will regard the idea as "preposterous" because "you don't do that", there will be no analogous restraint in Congo because the country lacks this kind of centuries-honed tradition. As such, <u>genius loci</u> or <u>genius tempori</u> either facilitate or impede actions of this type. On the other hand, once such actions "come about", it becomes quite difficult to radically break away from what is then a genocidal tradition. Society's task, I think, is to ensure that situations in which gainful perpetration of evil is possible cannot arise in the first place; simply put, people should not be exposed to coercion, temptation, or blackmail that only a select few individuals could ever resist. I must agree that the very existence of such exceptional individuals is startling and enigmatic. For example, the German Catholic who in 1943 (if memory serves) refused to join the Wehrmacht because he saw it and its war aims as "evil" — and Hitler as "evil" incarnate — was eventually executed even though his family, relatives, priests were all persuading him to "give in". In purely empirical terms, an individual behaving in such a singular manner is undoubtedly abnormal and aberrant; we are dealing here with a case of "moral pathology" which, for reasons that transcend the empirical ones, must perhaps be called morally "glorious" (meaning that, from the empirical standpoint, we are faced with a kind of <u>ne plus ultra</u>, as infrequent as premeditated murderers of

the sort represented by Jack the Ripper, only with
the opposite sign in terms of deviation from the
norm). Conclusions of this nature are perceived,
however, as considerably demoralizing and nihilistic,
so that, even though they are backed up by a wealth
of empirical evidence (from experimental psychology,
to say nothing of the annals of history), much of the
time they are not accorded due weight, which leads
to clashes when the matter comes up for debate — as
when Norman Podhoretz went head to head with Hannah
Arendt as to whether Nazis like Eichmann were quite
normal and average human beings (her thesis) or
rather evil monsters and demons (as he maintained).
In my opinion truth was entirely on her side. Also,
absence of a realistic alternative to what's going
on around facilitates the slide into genocide. This
is to say that, if a state functions under the
banner of "one true" doctrine or ideology — if a
hecatomb of torments is perpetrated in its name — if
there is nothing to appeal to outside the doctrine
— if there are no real physical people who could
form a tribunal of appeal — if there is not even a
possibility of seeking redress in a reflexive-moral
sense — then human lives become filled with nothing
but void. "Since there is nowhere to turn outside the
system, outside the party to which I also belong,
since there is nothing to look forward to except
execution — I will resign myself to the execution,
then." THIS type of a situation, crippling even
intrinsically bright minds, was far from infrequent;
after all, in the process of eliminating others,
the cadres of the persecutory apparatus would often
end up "feasting" on themselves, meaning that the
smarter among the directors and enforcers of these
persecutions must have realized that the next day
they were going to find themselves on the receiving
end of what they were dispensing today — yet this
reflection did not in any way impair the "efficiency
quotient" of their extermination campaigns! Whenever
any form of totalizing ideology takes over, it is no
longer even possible to indulge in the gesture of
Pilate — the shrug of resigned indifference, this

"come what may, I'm going to stay away from all this" — simply because this kind of gesture presumes the existence of some kind of asylum, of neutral ground, of a place where you can be indifferent, where you can retreat into escapism. Well, in general, in "proper" totalitarianism you could not find any such place (it couldn't be a convent, since those were abolished; it couldn't be a private country estate, since those were abolished as well; just about the only place like this might be among wolves in the forest, although not everyone is so fond of forests and of wolves-our-saviours). Turn things upside down, on the other hand, and you've got — this is funny, in its own way — students who see themselves being victimized by the methods of the Gestapo if you forbid them to mate with goats in public, to walk on their eyebrows, or to whistle down professors who are not to their liking, and then in a flash you've got arson, petards being hoisted, and such like. The essence of the machinery of totalitarianism is to crush the spontaneity of all dissent, opposition, revolt — whether rationalized or reflexive — IN THE BUD, in other words to create a mentality in which people are ready to queue for four days and night to get tickets to the circus or to sacrifice half of their lives just to buy a pair of undergarments. For, were such hardships to give rise to turmoil, riots, feelings of dispossession, it might lay bare the inefficiency of this particular form of totalism. When released officially by the state, all kinds of idiocies, the most outrageous nonsense should be accepted willingly and without question, even if it proclaimed that people are made of butter and cheese, that they think by means of dumplings, and that their goal in life is the pursuit of oak-stuffed cabbage (Koestler knew this very well writing Darkness at Noon).

[...]

You asked for my predictions for next year. Same as now, only a shade worse (higher inflation, greater world hunger, greater shortages of raw materials) but not yet to the extent that the world will be threatened with collapse. Your Nihilistic Monster is most likely not going to be **"impeached"**, unless of course (quod deus perdere vult, prius dementat)⁴⁴ he himself "crowns" the pile of his abominations with something that both chambers of Congress will not be able to stand. There is a possibility of new kinds of crises, among others due to friction within the body of the European Community. No chance for any sort of disarmament. Continued shortages of paper (higher prices of newspapers and books). Deterioration of global climatic patterns.

[...]

****

Cracow, 3 September 1974

[...]

There remains a question: if things are so gloomy and awful, why did I choose — and why do I choose — to write about them in the "lighthearted" mode? My god, because if I kept saying one and the selfsame thing over and over, nobody would want to read me! The more harrowing the content, the more comically it has to be dished out, the more basted with rib-tickling gravy, to turn it into a sort of counterpoint — in order to make bearable what cannot be borne at all.

[...]

****

⁴⁴ Latin: "whomever god wishes to destroy, he will first make insane".

Cracow, 23 September 1974

[...]

If I were you writing about me, I'd try to take the transcendent rather than the immanent tack; meaning, I'd write about PROBLEMS, each time correlating them with the specific treatment in my books (which is to say, I would move from problems to books, not the other way round). This way you can objectify the analysis and demonstrate both the strengths and the weaknesses of the author. For instance: the relation between culture and instrumentalism. Or, put differently: intelligent and stupid uses of science (or technology). If at first NOTHING is done for a long time and then, in the face of a crisis, humanity calls on science like it was a fire brigade, then science is left with almost no room to manoeuvre: working, then, with a very narrow focus it will likely manage to open SOME escape routes from the crisis, but these same escape routes may later on lead to other frightful crises (to take one example, if nothing is done about the demographic explosion, later on the necessary response will precisely be a STUPID use of science's instrumental potential). There are various ways of approaching this problem (most generally, perhaps, as a coefficient of the proactive anticipation of the future: a _wise man_ anticipates possible development way ahead of time, an _idiot_ only at the last minute — hence the former has at his disposal an array of technological strategies and the latter only desperate means — precisely à la fire brigade). Naturally, this is just an example; I only wanted to demonstrate that the kind of approach I'm talking about allows one to go beyond the traditional hopeless type of humanistic/literary-critical offerings (vide: the book by David Ketterer, with a chapter on _Solaris_ — well, nothing cognitively interesting flows from such intelligent psychoanalytic rinse-water).

[...]

****

Cracow, 2 October 1974

[...]

The flaw in your reasoning concerning the living in a totalitarian state is as follows. You cannot anticipate all the possible hardships and bad results caused by your decision of today, since there exists no known matrix of "payment" in such a situation: the official law must not of course say a single word about all the real harassments, awaiting the nonconformist. You must simply do what you think to be the best or the worst of the given case, and the rest belongs to the general unpredictability of all possible following events. No total rationalization is therefore possible. From other similar cases you will not extract any definite knowledge, since the situation being what it is, no case is truly similar to another; so there you have the free place for the play of imagination, and even if you will experience some unpleasant event, you will not be 100% sure, that THIS is the obvious result of your being nonconformist yesterday. This unpleasant event can be a pure coincidence too. Because of this, you can never be ABSOLUTELY CERTAIN of anything. **The less terrible the threat, the more we tend to judge a man who buckles under — <u>you say</u>. But this threat is always to an unknown degree determined by your subjective evaluation of the situation.**

[...]

****

Cracow-Frankfurt, October 1974

[...]

I'm taking advantage of my stay in Frankfurt to post a letter that will not be opened and read in Poland. Please treat the remarks contained herein as confidential; i.e., please do not release them, nor my name nor the place, into the public domain. I want to return to the matter of living in a totalitarian state, and knowing my own situation best, I intend to use it as an example. First of all, of course, I cannot express my real opinions about the difficulties in the part of the world where I live either in literary works or in monographs. I can skirt what's censorable by a whisker, but when I cross the borderline, as I do sometimes, they confiscate what I've written. This is no more than the banal reality of which I'm sure you must be aware. Next, I am aware that the correspondence that arrives here as well as the letters I send out are opened and read. This precipitates, among others, the massive delays in delivery that both of us have noted. Two years ago I was paid a visit by NUMBER THREE in the Politburo — who stressed during a private conversation that the contributions I had made to the promulgation of Polish culture abroad were now being "appreciated" and declared that from now on the "relevant factors" will systematically and concertedly support my candidacy for the Nobel Prize. He encouraged me to contact him in the event of any difficulty with publications, and so on. A year later, in the course of covert machinations within the party, Number Three "fell overboard". Officially no one knows anything about it. He simply disappeared from newspaper columns, he's not seen any more at party and state celebrations, etc. The reasons behind this de facto fadeout are not known, although there are, of course, any number of conjectures and rumours, e.g., that he somehow tried to shore up Poland's sovereignty vis-à-vis the USSR and that the blow

that felled him came from over there. On the other
hand, those could only be rumours spread by him
or by his concealed adherents! (In order, say, to
turn him into a "martyr of Polish independence"
and in this way increase his popularity). What were
the after-effects of his "fadeout" on my affairs?
On the face of it nothing seems to have changed at
all. Even so, I can tell that my books have been
taking longer to print since then than they used
to. The 1974 State Prize for which I was nominated
by my Cracow publisher went to somebody else.
Everything is going more or less like before, only
with a little more difficulty. Significant delays in
contracting new books, while the old ones are being
reprinted but very slowly. Previously publishers
used to contact me on their own all the time with
suggestions for reprints of sold-out editions.
They still do, but more seldom. And all this,
let's keep in mind, because of this "highly placed
feudal protection" for which I did not ask and made
no effort to obtain, much as I made no effort to
promote my candidacy for the Nobel Prize. At the
moment all sources are mum about the Prize, as if
not a word had ever been mentioned about it. In the
end, although I was not personally involved in any
reshuffles within the party, the very fact of the
"downfall of a powerful patron" — whom I did not
want and did not seek — has had a tangible effect
on my life. (So far <u>Imaginary Magnitude</u> received all
of TWO brief reviews in the entire Polish press).
And in the old days, during Gomułka's[45] regime, when
together with 30 of my colleagues I signed a letter
protesting the party's cultural policy? Nothing
DIRECTLY happened. Simply, I started to experience
bureaucratic difficulties, procrastinations, delays,
as a result of which I could not leave the country
for some time. I was never refused a passport,
it just so happened that whenever I was invited
somewhere, the passport would arrive too late to
take advantage of the invitation. Still, despite

---

[45] Władysław Gomułka, First Secretary of the Party (PZPR) 1956–1970.

everything, two years later I received a state decoration. I was (and now I am again) tolerated and left alone. The surge of "goodwill" from the authorities manifests itself in the form of increased interest from television, radio, film, a growing number of interviews, invitations to various public events, prizes, multiple reviews, doors opening, lucrative opportunities.

[...]

These days a relative liberalism, a kind of pragmatism, is in the air. The censorship even allows remarks to the effect that a book by a certain writer reveals his disillusionment with communist ideas! A generalized opinion of this sort can now be published; on the other hand, there is no chance of going public with even a single word against Russia. The entire topic is for us a sacred taboo. Moreover, we do not know and, given the circumstances, will never know whether this state of affairs is permanent, what are the actual limits of publishability, what are the concrete consequences of overstepping these limits, what the situation will look like in half a year, in a year, etc. What is today looked upon with impunity may one day yet become the basis for repressive steps taken against you. But, as it should be apparent from what I said before, repression is not confined to incarceration. When it's economic in character, it may actually be difficult to notice, but let's not forget that every single venue for publication is the property of the state. As such, signing the afore-mentioned protest letter I had no means whatever of knowing whether I was going to suffer any ill consequences, and if so, what kind. The unwritten law that governs here is capricious; it's a law of favours and disfavours, a lex ad hominem, so that what one person (for example, me) gets away with scot-free may have a very different outcome for another. It ought to be clear that, even though there is no danger of being tossed in jail, de facto you are looking in

the face of total starvation once your writing gets
prohibited COVERTLY (as befell a certain literary
critic who allegedly sullied and demeaned Russia
by means of allusions in his article on Dostoyevsky
— never mind that he was writing about TSARIST
Russia!!) because you will never eke out a living as
a **freelance writer** when from one day to another ALL
publishing houses, presses, and **mass media** close
their doors in your face. (It used to be that such
a person could be helped by his friends who would
publish his works under their names or by editors
who would take a chance and publish them under a
pseudonym, but this may have dire consequences
for everyone involved, although once again NO ONE
KNOWS IN ADVANCE WHAT THESE CONSEQUENCES MAY BE).
Right now, I repeat, we're in the middle of a period
of rather significant indulgence, of considerable
"freedom" and "benignness". But this system of
"privileges" can always be called off the next day,
all the more so that when it is in place, like now,
it relies on UNWRITTEN consent and on an unartic-
ulated assurance (what is de facto taking place can
contradict official policy to an arbitrary degree).
Surrounded by this murkiness, there is no point in
pursuing any kind of rational tactics, i.e., keeping
track of debits and credits, balancing the benefits
and drawbacks, calculating how far you dare to
stick your neck out and at what point it's better to
toe the line if you don't want to expose yourself
and your family to a sudden out-and-out ostracism,
a prohibition to reprint, to publish — all the
more so that, unlike a formal court sentence,
such a prohibition is always open-ended, so you
don't know if it's going to last three months, or
perhaps three years... In the end, as you see, there
is nary a need to put a gun to anybody's head if
results sought by the authorities can be secured
by innocent-looking methods that will not provoke
an outcry in the foreign press! I don't know myself
how much of the difficulties I have experienced
after "my patron's downfall" are a consequence of
having been lumped with the cadre of this "trendy"

politician's protégés and how much is the result of ordinary mess, editorial difficulties precipitated by paper shortages, etc. How can a tactical calculus even be possible in these circumstances? Let me add that I have no idea whether the lectures I gave for a year at the Jagiellonian University had been offered to me because the rector — aware that I received a visitation from Number Three — wanted to display his party zeal so he found an opening for the latter's protégé, i.e., me. All I know is that "accidentally" the termination of my lectures coincided with the downfall of that politician. Was it coincidence? A causal chain? God only knows! And all this, keep in mind, going on in the period of "thaw" and benignity...

[...]

****

Cracow, 18 October 1974

[...]

Regarding artistic matters, I don't remember if I mentioned R. Nudelman's[46] interesting observation about the structure of my novels which, he maintains, typically contain a "micromodel" of their problematics (the solaristic library in Solaris, "the mystery of the landlords" that bedevils detective Gregory in The Investigation, the concentration camp-like "selection of robots" in Return From the Stars). The method of construction has changed in my latest two books, A Perfect Vacuum and Imaginary Magnitude: Nudelman calls this new principle a spiral with a centrifugal momentum (where, semantically speaking, the first texts in both books are more "local and

---

[46] Rafail Nudelman, Soviet critic.

particular", while the last ones always reach for "the limits of being", as in "The New Cosmogony" in A Perfect Vacuum and in Golem's lecture on man in Imaginary Magnitude). Be that as it may, it remains a complete mystery to me why the problem driving Solaris preoccupies me so much that I returned to it for a second take in "The Mask". (This problem is, I think, the ultimate nature of the Creator's relation to the created Being, somewhat à la Wiener's last book, God and Golem Inc.). With the passing of years, certain strictly formal, compositionally almost musical, values have begun to play a prominent role in my mind. That's why — to take an example — Memoirs Found in a Bathtub features passages (in the conversation between Father Orfini and the protagonist) written in blank verse (which can be easily confirmed by reading those parts aloud in Polish); that's why in Illusions of Grandeur[47] I tried to hint at Golem's "illusions of grandeur" at certain moments in the prefatory sections, more or less like a main theme of a musical composition may be cued "ahead of time" before it makes an appearance fortissimo (hence, at the end of the day, my dissatisfaction with my older books, such as Return From the Stars or Eden). From the number of things to which I would very much like to draw your attention, I will enumerate here two. The "Metafuturological Conclusion" in the 2nd edition of Science Fiction and Futurology expresses my conception of Man — rather close to Golem's — which conception, as I found out only recently, has been thought up (or at least published in a pretty similar version) several years ago in West Germany by an author whose name I can't recall but which I'll send to you when I stumble on it again. (I'm not familiar with his works, only with their précis in Prof. Suchodolski's book published here in August '74). Next, I see an uncanny similarity between a deliberately loony and absurd cosmogonic theory I

---

[47] Canonical *Imaginary Magnitude.*

worked into Tichy's 19th voyage and a wholly serious theory published in Nature by a certain American astrophysicist three years after I had finished my story. ("**Is the Universe a vacuum-fluctuation zero**" — Science News, Dec. 22, 1973, contains a summary of this author's work: Edward P. Tryon, Nature, Dec. 1973 — whereas my story was created in 1970 which is established by the date of the relevant edition of The Star Diaries). To me, all this seems instructive... not of a specific coincidence or anticipation, but of a certain quality of my mind and the way in which it functions.

[...]

These days I mainly find myself repulsing attacks from all the people who want to yoke me to inessential things. I received an offer to lecture at the Jagiellonian U, this time in the Philosophy Dept., teaching cybernetics in relation to philosophy and especially theory of knowledge. I refused! How can I do it if I wish to continue writing?

[...]

****

Cracow, 19 October 1974

[...]

To my mind, you can never 100% dissociate the Cognitive dimension from the Artistic. For example, Summa technologiae (NB., out in the third edition, with a new introduction, and a rather important one, I have to say) — anyway, Summa is better than The Philosophy of Chance because it's better written, better in literary terms. But if these parameters HAD TO be dissociated, I would have to put it like that: if you take the philosophical road, the most important thing is THE DESTINATION, and if you take the artistic, the most important thing is THE ROAD TAKEN. For example, poetry is "nothing but the road": a poem directs itself to nothing outside the language of expression, i.e., it offers no concrete revelations or conclusions — everything hangs on HOW it leads the reader on this journey — whereas, precisely insofar as referential prose has concrete things to stuff into our heads, the (linguistic) road becomes less essential. Stripped down to the basics, this road is, of course, a matter of composition, of selecting the point of view, etc. Or, to put it differently: in nonfiction the guiding principle is the INVARIANCE of the subject of discourse, whereas in art the guiding principle is the very protean nature of the subject because a change in the mode of delivery doesn't change what nonfiction is about, whereas in art a change in the point of view changes the nature of the subject (of course, such generalizations are perennially risky but I'm using them here ad usum Delphini,[48] as will become apparent in a moment).

Where the nature of nonfiction is to address itself to concrete issues — so that nonfiction that has nothing new to communicate or that doesn't introduce new methods of evaluating what is already known isn't worth much — art teems with novelties that, in strictly cognitive terms, are all fictive. In my own case, I have always strived to be DIFFERENT in both domains, i.e., not to repeat anything after anybody. So, unwittingly at first, I imported into my works structures (paradigms) from science (empiricism). (A small, albeit eloquent, example is the short story about Dragons of Probability[49] which necessarily forfeits some of its flavour for people who have never even once heard of quantum physics). It took me a terribly long time to realize — and it came as

---

[48] Latin: "for the use of the Dauphin"—bowdlerized or, more loosely, simplified.
[49] From *The Cyberiad*.

a bombshell (such is human — i.e., my own — naiveté) — that no one at all has been able to detect this trick of mine (importing scientific paradigms into NARRATIVES)!

To go back to the previous dichotomy, I would have to say that, while I always keep a firm grip on the cognitive aspects, i.e., I am conscious of them during writing, the compositional aspects more or less slip through my fingers: in a word, I'm in control of my problematics but NOT of the art part. THE LATTER is fuelled by my unconscious, my obsessions, abominations, animosities, drives, and other compulsions. I don't know why this should be so; I don't know why I had to return to the problematics of Solaris in "The Mask", even though I normally hate doing so (repeating myself).

SOME characteristics of my art stem inescapably from the Zeitgeist, from the spirit of our era, which doesn't leave as much room for radical innovation as for the baroque, i.e., for convoluted, persiflagistic, parodistic, ironic-grotesque variations on time-honoured themes endemic to art, appropriated long ago, and this is why, among other things, SF drives me into a rage by dint of what it is doing, namely, with a kind of animal earnestness (mit tierische Ernst), replaying over and over stuff that must — i.e., ought to — provoke gales of laughter, instead.

[...]

Now, when it comes to PHILOSOPHY, I am quite rational in my epistemology[50] and more or less explicit about it, but things are different when it comes to ontology, since I believe that in Ego ("I") human beings come face to face with an inexplicable mystery because, although physics, biology, and other empirical sciences can successfully explain the coming into being and the existence of "others", i.e., "third persons", you can be pretty sure that

---

[50] Lem uses a rare term "gnoseology".

they will NEVER succeed in explaining where "I" come from. Within the natural sciences there is no way to <u>get</u> from "them" to "me" since, by virtue of its "inescapability", "I" denotes a place existentially unique (one cannot leave one's "I", step outside of it), and FOR ME THE DEEPEST MYSTERY OF EXISTENCE IS BURIED RIGHT HERE, everything else is just the consequence of IT...

[...]

****

Cracow, 29 October 1974

[...]

As far as Darwin goes, I think you may have turned things upside down a bit. I agree with the first premise, at least when it comes to the so-called evolutionary progress: progress is precipitated by danger. No one would scratch unless they had an itch, Einstein used to say in the context of attempting to account for <u>what</u> had jumpstarted scientific progress. Our species has indeed been shaped by poverty, danger, and the necessity of <u>incessant</u> STRUGGLE. **Man is a fighter.** This is exactly the reason why he is so ambivalent — so **ambiguous:** he constantly <u>craves</u> to fight and he is always <u>sick of it</u>. Created to stand up to dangers, he both "likes it" and he "doesn't like it". Civilizational progress has always moved us <u>away from</u> danger, whereas culture oftentimes moves <u>toward</u> it (which is to say that, when civilization pampers us, we respond by spiking the cushions with thorns). This is true. But we're talking here about reciprocal attitudes, about a game played out between civilization and culture (which is to say that, what is fully rational in the former, need not be so in the latter: you cannot anti-rationally manufacture a TV set, but the CONTENT of the broadcasts may be as anti-rational as you please). This is, by the way, what lies behind all this nonsense in McLuhanism (**media are the message**). It's the other way round: **Media are the civilization — culture is the message**. But this is already going beyond Darwin, inasmuch as he didn't deal with the socializing extensions of evolution. His Nature lacks this **ambiguity**. Species have come into being without the gift of autorationalization and **self-reflexivity** — this is our privilege and our hump alone.

   The Sydney Morning Herald (Austr.) published an enthusiastic review of The Cyberiad and Memoirs Found in a Bathtub. Some Pole in those parts sent me the cutout (from 12.10.74). First a few generous words about me. Then: **"You must read these fables for their sending up of the entire computer fraternity by one of their own mob, and for the rare combination of sly wit and children's humour, which, though frequently verbal in character, brilliantly survives through the translation. Fabulous! Arabian Nights and Rabelais Mechanized!... When an intellect of Lem's calibre is posessed od superb literary talent, one can only shout it from the rooftops." Well, Sir, there you have it. A certain Mr. WILLIAM NOONAN is of this opinion.** You have to go all the way to Australia to hear things like this. (Only in the provinces do they still read books, chimes in my wife).

   I just dashed off a long essay on ESP for Culture. Now a very fashionable topic over here. I dealt with it (i.e., telepathy) a bit in 1947 in Cracow. There is something in it — but it ain't mind reading. Many things in heaven and earth that are undreamt of by philosophers, etc.

   In the NY Herald Tribune (**Paris ed.**) J. Reston wrote about Ford — I mean, the essence of it was — that he may not be an intellectual eagle but at least he is honest, and after Nixon this is VERY nice. **No Comments.** And according to Le Monde, France is getting ready for terrible times. On ne parle pas plus de l'abondance, mais de la survie seulement.[51] **SURVIVAL OF THE FITTEST**. England has a shortage of 500,000 tons of sugar. Over here, the Marxists don't write about it so as not to panic the population, in anticipation of the following chain reaction: if there are shortages even there, no time to lose over here in sprinting to the corner store and buying out every last bag of sugar! Meanwhile <u>Newsweek</u> reports a **Surge of Communism** in Western Europe. And some chief economist at the UN writes word for word what I wrote six years ago. Instead of experiencing satisfaction of having known ahead of time how things were going to turn out, I experience fatigue. Where the Left used to be in power (West Ger.), now the elections are carried by the Right (CDU in Hesse[52]). And where the Right is currently in office (e.g., Italy), they vote the Reds in. "You can do something for the Poles, but never with the Poles", margrave Wielopolski used to say (during the times of the tsar). If you change "Poles" for "people" in general, it works as well.

Yesterday they offered me lectures at the Jagiellonian U — foundations of futurology, so, futurology and theory of knowledge. 15 hours over one semester, Dept. of Philosophy. I agreed.

People always calling from Germany for an interview. Yesterday — radio West Berlin.

Also gave an interview for the Moscow <u>Literary Gazette</u>.

[...]

These days my son starts almost a book a day — he has his own typewriter. Of course, he writes PHONETICALLY — doesn't have too many ideas, keeps complaining about LACKING them!

Yesterday a field mouse came to winter with us, making a nest in my room — to the enormous relief of my wife who, for many years now, has been vainly

---

[51] One no longer speaks of abundance, only of survival (Lem's French error—double negative—in the original).
[52] Central-west province of Germany.

trying to rationally convince herself that mice are
<u>quite likeable</u>.
 So far, this mouse of mine has been behaving itself quite decently.

[...]

****

Cracow, 3 November 1974

[...]

Prepping for lectures at JU, I've recently paged through several textbooks on the history of philosophy and was struck by the growing (along the temporal axis) one-sidedness of ontological systems: the later they originate historically, the more partisan (**biased**) they are, in terms of asymmetrical distribution on the plane of all human knowledge. My own education is that of an omni-dilettante. I was drawn to biology already in high school: it's possible that even then I approached Man as a CONSTRUCT, even though I wasn't yet aware of the IDEA (which could have come to me from the books with which I was surrounded at home). I wrote about it in <u>Highcastle</u> — that, as a child, I delighted in going after forbidden books, chiefly the anatomical atlases and medical books of my father's. I had, after all, Meccano and other constructor toys to play with, and in these atlases the very sequentiality of osteology, mycology, and splanchnology[53] plainly pictured the CONSTRUCTION of a human being in the manner of a machine, from the skeleton all the way to the skin. My medical studies must have only reinforced this perception. Later, after the war, fate decreed that I found myself at the SCIENCE STUDY

---

[53] A study of, respectively, bones, muscles, and viscera.

CONSERVATORY in Cracow where I devoured all kinds
of publications in cybernetics while being inducted
into neopositivistic philosophy, the darling of my
then mentor, the founder of that Conservatory, Dr
Choynowski. Man as a construct determined by the
spectacular path of development taken by evolution
— even if only one of many equally possible,
i.e., by no means necessary — became for me a
self-evident notion. This is why now, coming across
the axioms of Husserl's philosophy (phenomenology),
so incredible in their apodictic naiveté, I can
only feel disbelief commingled with irritation
that anyone, absolutely anyone, who wishes to cloak
himself in the mantle of an ontological "thinker"
can by fiat design for himself a philosophical
system unencumbered by ANY prior considerations. Just as if a human mind could delimit
existence that is absolute, necessary, permanent,
ultimate, and most of all completely free of any
pre-programming and therefore somehow EMPTY, right
until the moment when the thinker sits down to
ponder the nature of existence and its attributes.
Whereas the whole point is, after all, whether
<u>nihil est in intellectu quod non fuerit prius in sensu</u>[54] really depends on a prior construction of
the thinking subject.

[...]

No one has ever tried to figure out the right place
for my books within the domain of POLISH literature.
You won't find my name even in the glosses to
the outlines of the history of national belles
lettres (which nowadays are published quite often,
actually). I'm listed neither with the opportunists
nor with the revisionists, nor with any other
identifiable currents. This is so, I think, because
for two hundred years now our literature has borne
the curse of immediacy: the immediacy of bringing

---

[54] Latin: "nothing is in the intellect that has no basis in the senses"—the key tenet of empiricism.

"the visible world to justice", the immediacy of "catching up to the West, beginning with Europe", the immediacy of "inventing something Polish, something new", the immediacy of "showering the new with flowers", the immediacy of demolishing or monumentalizing national myths...

[...]

****

Cracow, 15 November 1974

[...]

I'd like to write a second volume pendant to The Cyberiad, a kind of Electrodicy (after Theodicy, although I'm not saying it's the right title), a book that should surpass the previous one in complexity of ideas since I'm haunted by duplicitas casuum[55] (cf., Robotic Fables : The Cyberiad; A Perfect Vacuum : Imaginary Magnitude). The first thing I'd like to include in such a volume is a history of struggles to create beings designed to be mere tools fashioned for a specific purpose, but who eventually confront their creators with typically God-like dilemmas, such as: is it possible for a Creation to acquire powers equal to those of the Creator or not? (Democratic versus non-democratic variant — in every monotheism God has opted for the non-democratic variant, sugar-coated with Love-as-Grace in the Christian edition). Assuming the non-democratic principle of creation, should predestination (predetermination of will or ethics) block the road from the Creation to the Creator? (This is an interesting problem since, in order to block access to Himself, God has closed the access road — only SPECULATIVE to begin with! — with a postulate credo

---

[55] Latin: "doubling of things".

quia absurdum est[56]; meaning that He requires us to abandon rational reasoning in His presence). By that token He requires us to surrender what He had given us, and this is not nice, since: "He who gives and takes away rots in hell"[57]; so much so that, by demanding a sacrificial offering of Logic, God at the same time disrupts the Moral equilibrium between Himself and His Creation. In the case of my would-be Creators, I would like these dilemmas to manifest themselves in a totally natural, necessary manner. Then I'd like to show how they need to endow their Beings with emotional life, and what it leads to. (Sex!). Such are my daydreams.

[...]

RIAS (Radio im Amerikanischen Sektor) of West Berlin conducted a cable-radio interview with me that turned out to be an ugly cold-war attempt to cook up a political scandal. (Questions: "How do you imagine the transition from socialism to communism? Why did you drop Tichy's 26th Voyage from the subsequent editions of The Star Diaries?" Everything in this style). I wriggled like a wet eel but it wasn't pleasant. I came to realize, by the way, that even over here The Futurological Congress is regarded as a novel with a "Hood" (ugly reality covered up on the outside by beautiful but deceitful fiction). But this wasn't at all what I had in mind when I wrote it.

In SFS (Science-Fiction Studies), my essay demolishing Todorov's theory of the fantastic — well translated by Abernathy.

[...]

Superstitions, delusions, etc. From some point on I started to repeat after my father that in our family everything generally ends rather well,

---

[56] Latin: "I believe because it is absurd (irrational)".
[57] Polish proverb.

albeit <u>after countless complications</u>. If you consider my career, my marriage, my various bouts of illness, the statement seems to fall close to the truth. (My wife gave me the thumbs down the first time I proposed; renewed after 1.5 years, the suit gave better results). In the early days the national literary-critical establishment used to push me DOWNSTAIRS as a writer, toward juvenile entertainment, whereas nowadays I'm hoisted UPSTAIRS (that is, towards philosophy). At first what I did was NOT YET literature, and now it is NO LONGER — can you believe it? <u>Solaris</u> came out in French some 12 years ago: not even one lame dog took notice. And so on.

Undoubtedly, my writing habits are irrational to the point of being self-harmful: for years now I have stopped jotting down ideas that pop in my head, to my greatest detriment, since oftentimes I forget things. Is it a form of sacrifice to the Moirae? I don't know. But I never pack my typewriter in the case; instead, it's always standing "at the ready" — even when I'm not writing anything. It used to be that, leaving the house at night, I would leave the desk lamp on, seemingly to create an illusion of my being On Watch. I realize these are all innocuous details, and that it would be more <u>profitable</u> to report some horrible manias and lunacies! Only somehow I cannot dredge up any.

No doubt I'm emotionally cold and can't stand PHYSICAL contact with people (hugging old acquaintances not seen for years, for instance). But, at the same time, I've never been a stranger to passions; in bed, thinking about various irritating things in the middle of the night, I can drive myself into such a state that I can't fall sleep till the morning...

[...]

****

Cracow, 22 November 1974

[...]

I starred on a talk show on our TV, based on American programs (guest star in a crossfire of questions) — only, of course, the entire "barrage" was quite mild and gentle. They built a Moon for the show, tiny craters and all, and they had an old black ornate chair flanked by columns for me and giant meteoric boulders for the interlocutors. Then there was a review of "cosmic fashion" and, in the finale, a Red Elephant and a Telephone Handpiece with smoke pumping from it rode down from on high. The program, first in the series, was watched by everybody, i.e., "all Poland" (more than 4.5 million sets means practically everybody alive, except infants, blind people, and folks in hamlets where TV has not yet penetrated). Everyone saw it, which became clear in the following days (shop assistants, parking valets, gas station attendants, carpenter, gardener). Everyone liked it, too, even though not one of the reg'lar folks understood much from the questions <u>and</u> from the answers; they probably liked it on the same principle that people used to like the incomprehensible Latin mass better than the Polish one... Everything was pretty, colourful, on the Moon you could see enlargements of every single character from <u>The Cyberiad</u> (or rather Mróz's illustrations from the book). From the questions — the most sophisticated ones — I gather that practically no one approaches literature as <u>literature</u> and that, for the average Joe, there's no distinction whatsoever between somebody's real point of view — say, my real views on the world or on the future — and pseudo-views expressed in a literary work...

[...]

So, we've got this mouse upstairs and can't get rid of it, since it's a very crafty and effective creature, capable of giving the slip to every kind of snare, net, or trap. Aside from the mouse — we bought for ourselves, i.e., for the child, i.e., for ourselves a colour TV, so that now we sit and watch the most tedious Plenary Committees with interest for the <u>colour effects</u>... zits on foreheads... so <u>pretty</u> in pink... and the jackets and neckties on the gentlemen and the sweaters fashion on the ladies. Ours are modest, provincial amusements, dear Sir! In my thoughts, a Strange Idea, the world as God's Mask, things of this sort, but I don't know if it'll ever amount to anything.

[...]

****

Cracow, 29 November 1974

[...]

The simplest way to get to the heart of the matter is via my own "theory of resonances". Artworks resonating with readers UNISONO — i.e., those that synchronically actualize, verbalize, articulate the aura of contemporary beliefs (worldviews, attitudes, dreams, fears, excitements) — achieve success that is QUICK but, generally speaking, SHORT-LIVED (= **bestsellers**). The value of works that position themselves ahead of their readers by articulating what is already taking place, but what has not yet been conceptualized <u>explicité</u>, becomes recognized after a certain delay; this **time lag** is proportional, among other things, to their originality of expression. Simplifying things rather drastically: when <u>The Cyberiad</u> appeared on the market, the response from readers in Poland was microscopic. In time, however, people began to like the book: the CODE in which it is written became more widespread. The situation was similar, even if also different, with <u>Summa technologiae</u>. It used to be a "what is it", a curiosum, something manic — and now it is **self-evident,** almost completely trivial. And therein lies the difference between a belletristic and a nonfictional work. A nonfictional book ahead of its time — a precursor — must eventually grow stale, and there is no helping it, since the book does not really possess a code of its own with which to create a sort of closed Universum. In contrast, belletristic works are equipped with such a code and can create "worlds of their own" — as does <u>The Cyberiad</u>. (Therein also lies the essential difference in interpreting anticipatory nonfiction and creative fiction).

   It seems to me, as a matter of principle, that there may be works aiming at a system of resonance that has NEVER arisen, just because cultural evolution has moved down <u>other</u> roads, other paths. That is, there may be works that would have been hailed as works of genius, had the type of vision, analysis, or depiction of events they had tried to advance become the axiological norm of some specific historical period. (Which, indeed, implies that I regard any cultural path as evolutionarily "unnecessary", i.e., I allow that every culture may have had "other" variants that just never crossed from virtuality to historical actuality).

[...]

The changes taking place in the UN (resentment among developing countries visible, e.g., in the hatred of Israel or in "exposures of White Man's bias") are portentous and dangerous. Whatever you say about the Superpowers, at the end of the day they have always showed a modicum of moderation and restraint, which is to say that they have actually conducted themselves rationally even when they conducted themselves like monsters. On the other hand, the behaviour of the Newbies in the UN lacks, more than anything else, any trace of such considerations (i.e., that the world must go on, that tomorrow is not the last day on earth, nor in the year 2000, that after the current round of crises and dilemmas there will be new ones — in a word, that it's hopeless to hope for conclusive Once-And-For-All Solutions). (Is it because the UN is turning into a Crowd and becomes subject to the laws of the psychology of Crowds, as described already in the old days by Gustave Le Bon? Nah, that's too simplistic). In addition, I'm leafing through all kinds of books devoted to Global issues — for all the braininess, even reason and intelligence of the authors, I am struck by their mutual incompatibility, by the colossal spread of their opinions and points of view; one here, the other one there, this is brutally depressing... Only one common denominator: Fear.

[...]

Our poor mouse! The cat got it and made a meal of it, how's that for a thought.

[...]

****

Cracow, 7 December 1974

[...]

Accident as a singularity does not preclude regularity on a more general level. In systems such as the evolution of life on Earth, the evolution of styles in the visual arts, the evolution of genres and styles in literary prose and poetry, the evolution of ethnic languages, or the evolution of religious faiths, "lucky coincidences" bear on the repertoire of all possible combinations of elements in their datasets. After all, not all (in principle) possible combinations of constitutive elements

give rise to actual evolutionary systems that
potentiate continued development in the future.
In world history, perceived regularities have led
to the development of the concept of cyclicality
(Spengler, Sorokin, Toynbee) — notwithstanding the
fact that the schemata employed by these histori-
ographers are only primitive reflections of more
complex states of the matter. It is neither true
that a genius creates ex nihilo (a creator without
precursors) nor that a genius is dominated through
and through by existing stylistic patterns and
methods of creation. It is possible that, in the
absence of Shakespeare, the Elizabethan drama as
we know it would never have taken off in the first
place; on the other hand, there is no doubt that
there would have been no vacuum in its place, no
gaping hole, but rather something else — very likely
something stylistically similar, even if, without
doubt, completely different in the specifics of
the created works (such as those created by lesser
spirits who may have needed to effect the transformation only "in instalments"). The presumptuous
originality of my views stems entirely from the fact
that I see a higher unity of laws that govern such
far-flung systems as natural evolution, the evolution
of culture, the evolution of art — everything from
the history of animal species to the sociopolitical history of humankind. Evolution within
these domains is neither totally predetermined
nor totally formlessly unspecified. The haphazard
effects of particular accidents can either fortify
the overall process — enabling, for instance, a
coherent orthogenesis — or decelerate it, or even
derail altogether it by switching it at a critical
juncture onto a different track. The Gothic NEED
NOT have given way to the Baroque, but the ensuing
art-historical formation HAD TO be a Baroque of one
kind or another. Man NEED NOT have emerged as a
successor to simians but, given the conditions on
earth, some form of life of another HAD to embark
on the path of progressive encephalization and,
on its way, step over the threshold that separates

the animal kingdom from the realm of beings that
<u>must</u> go on acculturating themselves. No specific
human language HAD TO arise but, at the same time,
the predispositions inherent in the way in which
the hominid brain is shaped — which reflect the
conditions of existence going back to the first
groups that had undergone anthropogenesis — HAD
TO lead to the emergence of ethnic languages. We
could have ended up with a different assortment of
languages, but they would have been functionally
equivalent to those we actually have.

A singular mystery surrounds the pattern common
to all these processes, whereby we can always
distinguish the "<u>dawn</u>" (daybreak, initial indefi-
niteness of the inception phase) characterized
by only a minimal determination of subsequent
development; the <u>culmination</u> (the pinnacle
of developmental richness); and the <u>twilight</u>
(cessation, hyperadaptation, superfluity, repetition,
sophism, fatigue, and not least sterility). It is
as if every process of creation HAD TO pass through
these stages; they become readily visible if you
juxtapose the regularities of the natural evolution
of species, the historical evolution of cultures,
and within the latter the history of art, of faith,
etc.

Well, in terms of recognizing "mutations" or
"innovations", the practical conclusions from what
I said above are the same for all these domains.
Mammals coexisted with giant reptiles for tens
of millions of years as "Nature's temporarily
overlooked masterpiece"! Clearly, **time lag** can
arise at any point, and at any time, between
the birth of an innovation and its eventual
"recognition". Whether "innovative genius" WILL
always be recognized at the end of the day or
whether there may be cases of permanent oversight
is hard to say, since the evolution of any
system is always embedded (nested) in a specific
environment. If one were to assume environmental
conditions as incontestably GIVEN, then "neglected
geniuses" or "neglected evolutionary species" are

mooted from the get-go simply because a given TYPE of environmental boundary conditions — which act as a habitat to the said "innovation" — would have prevented their birth. But if one were to assume that the boundary conditions could have been different — different types of mountain formation, climatic changes, etc., in evolution; different types of sociopolitical development in the annals of world history; etc. (after all, there COULD HAVE BEEN a great array of differences!) — then, in a case like this, it is okay to say that the "chances of emergence of original genius" were latent in the given system, but have never become selected for and amplified.

The fact that SF exists, and the fact that it "sucks into itself" what I write, harms my career, of course, rather than boosts it. The differentiation of one type of writing from the other is, indeed, a source of difficulty for readers, all the more so that our times don't favour deep reflection in contacts with art... So, the question of whether "higher values in art are recognized" demands placing it in a broad context of matters such as those raised above, seemingly disconnected, distant... Undoubtedly, my belletristic stuff rhymes well with my philosophical works *et vice versa*, but... who nowadays spends his time intensely studying one and the other?

[...]

****

Cracow, 25 December 1974

[...]

I've got in my hands the French press (Figaro, Le Monde), the American press (Newsweek, Herald Tribune, sometimes the New Yorker, Daedalus), the

German press (Süddeutsche Zeitung), from time to
time I also glance at Paris Match. The overall
picture is quite eerie: grumbling, energy doom and
gloom, utter uncertainty (not to say ignorance)
dolled up in banal phraseology before being smudged
on the page in the printer's ink — and all this
interspaced with magical islands from an entirely
different world of large colourful advertisements,
promising just like in the old days utter happiness
and fulfilment upon the purchase of a refrig-
erator, automobile, baking powder or, in the case
of Playboy, vigorous but at the same time refined
pursuit of raunchiness. The Germans who, following
the last war, have regained neither top world
rank nor even the aspirations to regain it, are
nonetheless not as traumatized and upset as the
French, whom de Gaulle lulled to sleep with dreams
of power. What a contrast between their relatively
recent overweening pretensions to standing up to
both superpowers (but above all to America) and
sober reality, as part of which, even as they hide
behind old slogans, maintaining the sorry façade
of politics as usual, their politicians go visiting
the oil sheiks cap in hand, all this time dreading
American supremacy even more than they dread what
the sheiks are up to — specifically that, under
the pretext of forming a developed countries' bloc
against the sheiks, the United States may pull a
fast one by taking advantage of the whole situation
and aggrandizing itself to new heights of economic
and political world supremacy at France's expense.
This type of schizophrenia paralyzes the political
thinking of the French, who are still pining for
what is clearly and evidently no longer within
their reach, and who, from one moment to the next,
jump from discussing their chances of avoiding
the current crisis and the threat of collapse to
blathering about the magnificence of France and its
role in the world. I'm not saying — since I don't
know the answer myself — that the anxieties behind
the French anti-Americanism are entirely groundless
but, for all that, the elation that swept through

the French press after Ford and d'Estaing's meeting on Martinique would seem to herald some kind of authentic triumph, whereas the only thing that actually happened was that — even as it remained ambivalent about it — France discarded the shell of its isolation (the rest of the European Community is not much better). On the other hand, when it comes to any long-range political strategy to guide the West, there's still not a trace of it — even as statements put forth by sundry symposia as well as by persistently questioned economists, statesmen, and experts only expose the magnitude of their ignorance, their <u>lack</u> of conceptual tools to deal with this new-fangled situation, while, at the same time, the voluminous efforts of futurologists past and present are (quite rightly, in most cases) ignored as effectively as if they had never existed at all.

[...]

****

Cracow, 9 January 1975

[...]

The charge levelled at me in Poland — though not as sharply or as clearly as in my paraphrase — alleges that, with titles such as <u>Imaginary Magnitude</u>, I'm overstepping the limits of belles letters, producing etudes from, let's say, the realm of philosophy or essay writing or fantastic (or semi-fantastic) historiography, but <u>not works of literature</u>. My answer to this is as follows: what was perceived yesterday as a transcendence of the limits of belles letters may <u>today</u> constitute an integral part of literary art; insofar as the limits in question are by nature impermanent, they depend on accepted conventions, so that, <u>following a change in the</u>

<u>latter</u>, fantastic philosophy or theology may become, precisely, the belletristic "norm".

[...]

****

Cracow, 23 January 1975

[...]

Determinism and indeterminism — when you start to think deeply about this opposition, what could be more fundamental and yet bring with it so many problems? (Singular occurrences versus only statistical regularities, etc.) Take history — isn't it, above all, **"sound and fury"**, a chaotic tug-of-war basted with the gory gravy of humankind's blind savagery? But as soon as you say that, you have to contend with postulates of perfect regularity originating at the other end of the spectrum, so to say. Most often, however, overarching syntheses — these "wholistic" perspectives on mountainous anthills of events — are characterized by an overall coherence (**Gestalt quality**) and an alluring clarity when viewed from afar, just like distant mountains on the horizon are integrated into perfect unity by virtue of being distant which smears out all constituent detail, so much so that it is only when you begin to walk toward them that their perfect, unified shape dissolves into all kinds of chaos. (Or: viewed from afar, the lunar disk resembles nothing so much as a geometry of crater rims and circles, whereas the closer you approach, the more this uniformity — this common geometric denominator of the Moon's surface sculptures — begins to dissolve, so that, after landing, once again you perceive nothing but chaotic accumulations of fissured clumps of rock.) Evolution of any kind seems to exhibit a curious oscillation along the temporal axis. I'm

talking about fluctuations — either self-induced or
introduced externally. More than anything else,
we perceive evolution as either self-steering and
autonomous or as externally guided, impelled and
steered by factors external to itself. The synthesis
of this polarity — which, in my opinion, arises out
of our perceptual deficiencies — is for now supremely
difficult. Why do cultures fluctuate in this way, just
like nature's species or phyla? Why do they exhibit
maximums and minimums in the rate of evolutionary
change? Why doesn't the infinite — or the PRACTICAL
infinite — of all possible permutations and
combinations of every assembly-kit present at the
inception of every evolutionary process support
continuous ascent? Why does their domain — their
paradigm — turn out to exhaust itself so easily?
Why does CYCLICALITY so persistently dominate nature
and culture — biology and religiosity? Why exactly
should the laws of CONSTRUCTION of all living
beings, from trilobites to humans, be similar to
the laws of "construction" in culture — especially
in the domain of language — if everything over
there is constructed out of matter and over here
out of concepts, if everything over there is "flesh"
and over here "spirit"? Oh no, there's no way all
this can be somehow explained away as self-evident
because, if we blandly assume that there exists only
one Cosmos with only one set of laws, and that by
this very token every subset of it — whether anthro-
pogenetic or language-genetic — ought to exhibit
analogical traits, we fall into a pretty nasty trap
just because, if all of this were true, it would
negate even the possibility of understanding why
there are idiots and sages in the world (since the
laws are uniform, everything that is the outcome
of these laws ought to be like everything else).
To my mind, investigations of differences between
genuine kinships displayed by "wholistic" phenomena
and their merely superficial analogues are a litmus
test of ontological inquiries — and a rock on which
it is all too easy to crack one's teeth. Perhaps you
might be inclined to quickly nod your assent at this

point — not so much from the deep conviction that, by virtue of his perspicacity, Lem has gnawed his way into the very nucleus of the nature of Being, but from considerations of a conversational-social-amicable type, as one is wont in conversations with a dude like me who is prone to maniacal obsessions... After all, it's nobody's secret that the formidable, centuries-old efforts perpetually renewed by philosophers can never be crowned with concrete, conclusive results, as attested by the multitudinousness of the aggressively contradictory results of their Sisyphean labours. But if this is so — and, really, is there anyone outside the dogmatists who doubts it? — a thought presents itself that, since no one can be ultimately right (or, if so, one doubtless couldn't prove it) — is there really any big difference between this or that ontology...? And once you accept this, it's easy to take these conceptual struggles over the nature of the world for granted, in the end shading into nihilism — naturally, not the gold-plated philosophical kind (self-destructive, fiery, intense, destructively aggressive) but its tame variety: mild, genial towards the whole world, purely pragmatic, and as such somehow innocent and even, in practical terms, likeable. From the latter's point of view, all philosophy is maniacal toil that condemns its victims to a variety of torments which are as imaginary (since self-induced) as the manias that had triggered them in the first place, being simply — in terms of our culture and its conventions — syndromes of undiluted pathology. So, from the frying pan into the fire.

Up till now we've had no winter at all, so everyone is starting to doubt whether it's ever going to report for duty. No doubt we'll have to pay for it with an odious, sleety, cold summer, same as these last few years.

[...]

****

Cracow, 4 February 1975

[...]

The French translation of The Cyberiad is, to put it plainly, utterly wretched — a complete antithesis to your Cyberiad, because rendered without all the jokes, especially the linguistic ones, and as such riddled with utter nonsense, idiotism, malarkey; I couldn't make myself thumb through this French je ne sais quoi to the end. Yet, despite this, it actually keeps selling... and, to be honest, no better and no worse than your translation, as is apparent from the balance sheet I got yesterday from the firm DENOEL... Moving on. Now that I'm "**in**" in West Germany, each of my books released successively over there receives by and large concise, repetitious, but invariably positive — not to say highly laudatory — reviews, particularly in the daily press (in columns that recommend to readers books WORTH READING). Lately, precisely in this choral manner, they have been raving over Return From the Stars. At the same time, Mr. Ivansky from Chicago — I'd written about him before — sent me a Xerox copy of a rejection letter from DOUBLEDAY regarding his translation of Return From the Stars. The letter states that the book is awfully BORING, that it isn't **fast paced**, that it's about 100 pages too long, and that it doesn't meet any of the "criteria expected of good Science Fiction". Can't argue with the facts — and over the years a multitude of such facts crossed my field of vision, corroborating the accuracy of my view on the RECOGNITION OF VALUE of literary works — a view that happens to be diametrically opposed to what lit-crit humanists, experts, and other theoretically learned souls profess. To wit, I believe that the process by means of which a community of readers accepts the sort of book that doesn't kowtow to readymade schemas of this or that literary genre has, for all practical purposes, nothing to do with what goes on in the head of every individual

<u>in question</u>. For — and this is a rather straight-forward matter — VALUES do not get recognized in the same manner that cupboards, clouds, taborets, and stones do; rather, they manifest themselves to readers when readers have already been persuaded <u>in advance</u>, so to say, of their presence... In other words, we're talking about mass-statistical phenomena that correspond either to a reaction that takes place during diffusion or osmosis in a colloid or to a process that takes the form of a "chain reaction" in a lump of uranium. Generally speaking, the proper model of these phenomena is physical-chemical: PHASE transition with its <u>critical transition points</u> from one state to another. Once a phase transition takes place, it is practically <u>irreversible</u>. This means that, once an author has been "accepted", his subsequent books may be god-awful but, out of inertia, they will continue to be bought — he has become an integral part of the "cultural landscape", and that's it. The oddest factor here is the PACE of recognition of a book's (or books') originality. For all practical purposes, this PACE is almost independent of the exclamations of rapture, horror, or outrage with which literary experts inundate pages of relevant periodicals (T. Mann publicly extolled Musil's work; this helped Musil as much as incense candles help the dead). On the other hand, this pace is roughly proportional to the time a given book has been on the market and to the statistical <u>mean</u> of the sum total of critical opinion. Once the pace of recognition enjoys a kind of <u>acceleration</u>, the writer's status becomes fixed; he begins to "count", and from then on his "stock value" is safe from slipping into utter oblivion and total neglect. He doesn't even have to be read widely — it is enough that he is known, that from that point on his name and ECHOES of his works are in the SOCIAL DOMAIN.

If the pace of "acceptance" of a particular newcomer is high enough, the whole process begins to assume the character of AUTOCATALYSIS (the more the writer is talked and written about, the more he is talked and written about, so that knowing him acquires overtones of a cultural must). In any case, there's no need to read his books as long as you sport a few on your shelf and are capable of conversing about him. As a diagnosis, "snobbism" fails to explain anything here, especially that, if you posit that everyone is a snob, then — needless to say — no one is, insofar as snobbism is an attitude contrary to "nonsnobbism" (it's the same with beauty: if everyone was beautiful, no one would). From this it doesn't follow, of course, that the merit and the value of individual works are never recognized; on the contrary, such recognition does take place but, in terms of the entire domain of societal reception, its effect is so microscopic and it constitutes such a negligible margin that it simply doesn't count at all. This whole phenomenology is rather complicated: a work may become popular, yet never make the roster of classics, or it may achieve the rank of a classic but remain unread (notwithstanding the fact that it still affects culture by its mere presence: for example, by influencing other creators). To me, the strangest aspect of the pace of cultural recognition and status acquisition by writers and their works is that, as a rule, it is so sluggish. It looks for all the world like collective opinion does, indeed, accrete according to the laws of gradual diffusion and osmosis — like there is an original "nucleus" that emits informational molecules about the writer and the work, both of which form a kind of "front" which, with a differential velocity, penetrates the various layers (**strata**) of society. Ah, these things are frightfully complicated and, needless to say, reducing them to judgments such as that readers must be blind or idiots, etc., doesn't explain a thing. Instead, one should pay attention to factors that shape the collective mind. Christian influences, for example, can be detected even in places such as the USSR, where Christianity has found itself "in exile", ostracized and systematically targeted by propaganda wars. Yet, even those who combat it <u>are under the influence</u> — however diffuse — of Christianity as a collective disposition...

Long story short, literature innovates to the extent that it <u>advances</u> a novel view of the universal order of things, a novel attitude towards the human and transhuman world, <u>yet the very fact of articulating any such view</u> — not to even mention the question of <u>the nature of the novelty</u> that is being advanced — is recognized only very late in the day. In cases like this, the **time lag** is always enormous; hence, as a rule, the author's "final" artistic grade arrives only after his biological time has run its course... (And the fact that some individuals may diagnose and recognize quality <u>accurately and immediately (or quickly)</u> has zero — and I mean absolutely zero — bearing on the overall pace of the whole process as it unfolds in society).

As you see, cunning Lem has readied himself in advance for all — including the worst — kinds of reception of his books, since the more neglected they become now, the more accurately this is going to verify his theoretical hypotheses...

[...]

****

Cracow, 9 February 1975

[...]

Literature is always and without exception an <u>Argumentum ad Hominem</u> — and, moreover, an argument whose every justification is only a (critical) <u>secondary rationalization</u>. As we all know, there are books we <u>love and respect</u>, those we <u>love</u> but <u>don't respect</u>, others that we <u>respect</u> but <u>don't love</u>, and finally those that are <u>unloved and disrespected</u> in equal measure. (Take me for an example: in the first category I place books — NOT ALL, HOWEVER

— by Bertrand Russell; in the second, Simenon's; in the third, Kafka's; and in the fourth, to mention just one item, typical Science Fiction.) The same distinctions obtain in our contacts with other people. E.g., women! For instance, you can acknowledge that, in the light of physical and spiritual attributes, a certain woman may be WORTHY of love while, at the same time, remaining perfectly aware that you yourself could never fall in love with her. To the question WHY ever not, you might come up with a plethora of answers but all of them would always be secondary rationalizations of the initial attraction — or repulsion. An honest critic is someone who esteems and applauds only what he himself loves and admires with his whole heart; naturally, the distinction between the two routinely collapses in practice... When it comes to evaluating my own books, the key to my pronouncements consists in putting myself in the position of the READER. I re-read The Cyberiad, The Star Diaries, as well as Imaginary Magnitude and A Perfect Vacuum without wincing and usually find in them things that please me and make me want to read other books like them — IF ONLY THEY EXISTED. Solaris, oddly enough, I respect more than love — I can't even work up the enthusiasm to proofread new editions. In general, I esteem a type of fantasy that carries me, like a wing, outside what is already Established and Experienced, what is already cognitively assimilated — and the consideration of whether such transcendence of cognitive limits is accomplished by means of nonfiction ("fictive ontology", "teleology", "philosophy", "linguistics", and so on, and so forth) or by way of belles lettres (via grotesque or a "visionary assault") is for me merely a matter of TACTICS, and nothing else. This doesn't make me a precursor any more than it makes you a traditionalist; it doesn't mean that I'm way ahead and you're way behind; all it means is that I am an egoist, and that I write (and read) what interests me, what gives me pleasure (without analyzing the elementary components: how much aesthetic pleasure, how much cognitive, how much entertainment, how much despair). You could say I seek TRUTHS as pure instantiations of possibility (naturally, this is only in my subjective point of view), and I thus agree with those who maintain that, as I grow in erudition and knowledge, I make my strictly-speaking belletristic efforts progressively <u>more difficult</u> in comparison to the already established creative norm (<u>The Cyberiad</u>, <u>Solaris</u>) insofar as my hunger for originality and for — to some extent, at least — truth-driven <u>novelty</u> impels me with a greater force than "applied" considerations, such as compositional, stylistic, or any other.

So, to take an example, being rather similar in spirit to Prof. Hogarth from <u>His Master's Voice</u>, I'm not too closely attached to the sentimental-reminiscence value of <u>Highcastle</u>, so that the only fragment of this book that still brings me pleasure as a reader is the section on "documentarism" as a metaphor/parable depicting the initiation of a child into the life of society, introducing a child to a set of instrumental tools thanks to which it begins to participate in the spiritual life of humankind...

[...]

****

Cracow, 21 April 1975

[...]

Recently my wife and I have been doing a bit of housecleaning and, while at it, we counted the various editions of my books. I didn't realize — I had no idea — how incredibly gruelling and slow was the process of my fledging as a writer. Do you know that the first edition of <u>Summa technologiae</u> was barely 3,000 copies? <u>Robotic Fables</u> — 7,000? Yet, at the time, I was already rather well-known in

Poland; I had Solaris under my belt, all the Russian accolades, yet my books still endured such limited reception. Up to 10,000 copies, they'd sell out in no time, but when once or twice the publishers printed 20,000, you could see them languish in bookshops for a while. I also remember how they used to review The Cyberiad, ignorant at first of what it was about, how to approach it, how serious it was, how much of a joke, how much paydirt in this joke. The authoritative opinion declared that the book was dexterously executed, albeit really rather traditional, a cross between a cybernetic lexicon and fairy tales for children. Because, dear Sir, the connections, relationships, implications, and associations that affiliate an artwork with the heights of the intellectual-aesthetic-philosophical realm are not detected in the same way that cupboards and taborets are. Before the Reader even allows himself to contemplate any such Venerable Affiliation, he must first obtain Permission from the Authoritative Areopagus. Things have to be cooking before then, the heat has to be turned on by guarantees from numerous of COMPETENT venerators, discoverers, hermeneuticians that "This is It".

[...]

There is one more significant factor that should eventually bring converts to my credo. To my mind, my books have a greater impact as a sum total, as a whole, than as individual titles. You may likely not agree with me on this point, but that's exactly how I see it. The igneous core of my books does not reside in the traditional rationalism à la Voltaire, or in affiliations with Swift, or in similarities with Kafka (or Gombrowicz) — all of which happen to be most easily spotted by literary critics. Instead, their nucleus is occupied by a paradigm entirely alien to art: patterns of thought characteristic of the bio-sciences. They are the same in every book, only their "mode" is different in the assorted grotesques, different again in the various typical "science fictions", and different still in works such as <u>Memoirs Found in a Bathtub</u> or <u>Imaginary Magnitude</u>. While all these modes are undoubtedly highly <u>divergent</u>, they always recombine in an almost identical <u>essence</u> which is <u>ontological</u>, rather than <u>political</u> or sociocritical, in nature. My art rides into battle <u>precisely</u> where scientific sources begin to reveal their <u>inadequacy</u>, where the might of science turns out to be a trap or a labyrinth for the human spirit, where <u>Darwin indeed triumphs over Hegel</u> but in a Pyrrhic victory.

[...]

****

Cracow, 21 May 1975

[...]

I had this idea about a desacralized version of a pact with the devil. A thoroughly average guy, away from home, walking around a strange **city** spots among thousands of advertisements and neon signs one that promises Wish Fulfilment and, on a whim, climbs upstairs for the hell of it (it's nighttime, raining outside, he's a stranger with nothing to do), whereupon he finds himself in a tiny office, a bureau of a company that offers him a contract (SOMEHOW, I see, I started to sketch this thing here, albeit as a grotesque, <u>vide</u>: <u>A Perfect Vacuum</u>) that amounts to the following: employing means that shall remain imperceptible to the client, the company undertakes to remove every obstacle from his life path in perfect accordance with his stated wishes and, for the time being, without charging him any fees for the said <u>contract</u> since this is still a startup period, a trial phase, i.e., the anonymous Investor who is hiding behind this advertisement wishes to find out first whether large-scale investment will be profitable, so that first customers will be served <u>free of charge</u> as a kind of laboratory mice, and our hero is one such case. The contract is signed, on a lark, without any faith that it is worth anything at all, but soon his luck turns around, everything starts going his way, getting better and better, so much so that people the protagonist considers highly inconvenient begin to disappear... (they perish in accidents, leave town for who knows where, etc.). More and more this streak emboldens the protagonist who begins to break out, so to say, from his natural, inborn character type (he used to be rather modest, rather timid, rather passive) — until he begins to act so recklessly, so devil-may-care, that he ends up embroiled in some colossal, not to say criminal, problems, upon which he takes a trip back to that city to "check the fine print" on this whole thing, to see if it had been for real (and, indeed, it seems to him at times that the whole transaction was just a dream), where it turns out that no such company exists — or rather, it does but only as a sort of advertising agency, and, as for the employee who negotiated the "contract" with the protagonist, no one will even mention his name (i.e., you don't know if he existed at all, or if the hero has been suffering from paranoia in the wake of the original visit), and the hero begins to sink into a self-made abyss. Of course, it's possible that the company had simply decided that the business wasn't worth it and consequently backtracked on everything (this was to remain an <u>open</u> question). As you see, this is a free-market variant on Paradise and Hell (supply and demand, the offer and the price to pay).

[...]

****

Cracow, 15 September 1975

[...]

Everything is already messed up by the fact that the publisher has re-christened the characters in Solaris, turning SNAUT into SNOW, et cetera, even though it says nowhere that Snaut is English or, for that matter, American; well, then, why are foreign-sounding names essentially forbidden in America, what is this xenophobia, this intolerance and, to put it in general terms, linguistic fascism??? Of course, I'm kidding here, but you know what I mean. No American translation of Dostoyevsky would ever be permitted to change Raskolnikov to John Brown.

[...]

****

Cracow, 28 September 1975

[...]

Lately I have succumbed to intellectual laziness of sorts, or, I should better say, indifference. Soon after they flash through my mind, all new narrative as well as (so to say) "philosophical" ideas simply dissolve without a trace since, not having jotted them down, I lose them from memory. I wonder why I should feel that way and where it all comes from? Have I experienced too much or too little success? I think it might be something else. Quite often I run into my unattributed concepts, i.e., in statements made by various people, in books, in essays, without it being a matter of witting or unwitting plagiarism. Most of the time, it's not like someone steals ideas from my books and presents them as his own. I can prove it incontestably, since I run into them in foreign authors who are certain never to have read

me. It only happens because I arrived at certain
diagnoses (e.g., those related to the state of our
civilization) a few years ahead of sundry professional thinkers, and because I hazarded predictions
that have, in the meantime, become reality and, as
such, a banality — anonymous elements of common
knowledge. This is a strange process of erosion of my
labours — as if the world kept picking away at them
like a murder of crows, bit by bit pecking out all
the tastier crumbs to claim for its own. At the same
time, it becomes a kind of **challenge,** a dare: if
you were so right, if 5, 10, 15 years ago you could
sense what is now plain to see and common, then
go ahead, do it again, foretell the next future...
but then comes a fundamental question, WHAT FOR?
Just so this process can go on like before, just so
it repeats itself? Recently, for instance, people
around here took to quoting some French literary
theorist cum philosopher as if they'd made a weighty
intellectual discovery all because back in 1971 he
proposed the same theses on the nature of a literary
work and its function in our times that I had
published in 1968 in The Philosophy of Chance. The
resemblance is striking. Well, the initial reflex is,
naturally, to write a letter to the publisher with
a relevant citation of my original formulations and
seek acknowledgment of my antecedence, of my precursorship, etc. But, of course, I did not even lift
a finger, what for? If only it was the first time...
but these things happen all too frequently, so —
what, I'm supposed to mount a systematic campaign
to "rectify" such errors, shouting nonstop that "I
WAS FIRST!"? It would be stupid and, in my view,
improper. But this indifference has spread to other
parts of me, so that now I'm thinking, okay, I could
certainly develop this or that idea into a book but,
ultimately, WHAT FOR? Humanity, stuck in fast-forward
on a global scale, is fundamentally inert —
everything in today's culture is so chaotic that all
attempts to tame this chaos are futile, including
the pretensions that one might have things to say to
the world like the Evangelists did...

I'm writing this from my den, my "hole", but far from crushed by depression — I'm rather serene, actually. In the end (I'm thinking to myself), are my books — this life of mine committed to print — so important? Can one at all attribute to literature the kind of value that could justify existence?

[...]

****

Cracow, 4 November 1975

[...]

I'm currently writing the last part of <u>The Chain of Chance</u>[58] and I've run into atypical problems, since this thing is constructed on the principle of a time bomb with a delayed-action fuse, and the course of events should create the impression of being not in the least predetermined. This is actually the most difficult kind of book for me (neither comical nor profoundly philosophical nor essayistic nor overly fantastic). It may yet turn out to be lousy, but certainly not uninteresting, in a more lowbrow sense. Ah, it has truly been said that, when it comes to writing, litterateurs are insufferable in their monumental exhibitionism.

[...]

****

---

[58] The Polish title, *Katar*, means *Runny Nose* (or *A Cold*); see Swirski, *From Lowbrow to Nobrow* (2005), Chapter Six.

Cracow, 8 December 1975

[...]

Several days ago I finished my novel — a **long short story**, really — The Chain of Chance, which is now being retyped clean while I'm enjoying a momentary breath of lovely freedom. I like this pleasant sensation of regaining my liberty which, I know from experience, very swiftly will succumb to the feeling of idleness. For the time being, though, I'm satisfied with the book, even though it's not any kind of breakthrough in terms of prospects for fame but rather something I wanted to write — so I did. I doubt, in all honesty, that you're going to like it. But, how tedious life would be if our preferences coincided to a tee with the opinions and judgments of those around us! I had finished the book in blood, sweat, and tears, and several times had a feeling like I was NEVER going to make it since — out of contrariness typical of me — I had chosen for the protagonist a guy who is in almost every respect dissimilar to me. But I think it all came out right in the end.

[...]

****

Cracow, 9 February 1976

[...]

As I have heard from Dr. Rottensteiner,[59] and as I could see with my own eyes in the SFWA newsletter, I stirred up quite a lot of bad blood over there, especially with my article published last year in Frankfurter Allgemeine Zeitung which the newsletter

---

[59] Lem's then literary agent outside Poland.

reprinted in translation. One Swedish **"fan"** by the name of Lundwall wrote to Rottensteiner (among others) that, according to his sources, I was allegedly to attend some **"con"**[60] in the States where I was going to get my comeuppance for the insults with which I dared to sully the enlightened SF. This is all gossip, but I have also heard that they are thinking of "taking away" my honorary membership of SFWA. I realize now — and not for the first time either — that it was stupid of me to accept that membership out of politeness when it was proffered. I'm also convinced — though I could be wrong — that, in terms of its policy regarding publication and publicity of my books, Seabury[61] prefers not to say goodbye to the supposed privileges entailed by the label of "SF" since, as I've observed in the new catalogue, they keep quoting again and again the same old endorsement — by T. Sturgeon, whom I regard as a hack and who must be regarded as a hack by any decent critic who knows his metier. Perhaps Seabury is under the impression that Sturgeon's name means something and wields some influence in the circles of SF readers, whereas the name of Arthur Koestler[62] means nothing and carries no weight in these same circles. I think this policy makes no sense either in terms of Fame or in terms of Fortune. If someone was to PROMOTE ME AS a writer of SF, he should bring out books such as <u>Eden</u> (as a last resort, <u>Imaginary Magnitude</u>) or <u>Return From the Stars</u> but not <u>The Star Diaries</u>, because, as I can see for myself from reading countless fanzines, a primitive reader of SF craves a **"sense of wonder"** while remaining insensitive to humour and comedy, being especially resistant to satire and grotesque, insofar as they presume certain sophistication and literary taste — or, to put it in lay terms, a measure of intelligence.

[...]

---

[60] Short for "convention".
[61] Then Lem's American publisher.
[62] Author of classics such as *Darkness at Noon* and *The God That Failed*.

Cracow, 26 February 1976

[...]

I don't know about you, but I can't write when I'm depressed (a state, for me, Far from Exceptional), and when I force myself to, out of Discipline, Honour, etc., nothing comes out of it. Liquor? Hmm! Naturally, I hit the bottle now and then, and only realize HOW MUCH when I go downstairs to the cellar — if we ever hit the hard times, the sale of these empty bottles will secure us a comfortable life for quite a while, they are So Many.

[...]

I've just re-read Popper's **Open Society and his enemies** — if you don't know it, I recommend it, written 25 years ago but as fresh as if it was today. A wonderful dismantling of Plato, Marx, and Hegel.

[...]

****

Cracow, 16 March 1976

[...]

Playboy (German edition) wanted to pay me $1,000 (DM 2,500) for a 10–12 page story, but I refused. Not that I have anything against female behinds, especially pretty ones, but I've got nothing currently ready and I don't want to write when someone is "calling the tune", no matter who it might be.

[...]

Cracow, 11 April 1976

[...]

One mustn't soar too high above readers' expectations of literary-critical norms nor stoop too low. If you're too high, you won't register on the radar, and if too low, they'll ignore you. There is an irreducible element of chance, of **randomness,** in the process of evaluating a literary Work which, I am practically certain, is a priori irreducible. No matter what, today you can't shock people any more, for example with a startling Scream-Roar that purports to be an Artwork. The norm predicts, after all, nominal departures from the norm — which is, by the way, a complete misunderstanding, an automystification on the part of the Augurs.[63] Problem is, the incompetence on the part of the Augurs increases exponentially in proportion to the increase in the menacing weight of all the world's problems — only they remain oblivious to the problem, and wouldn't even recognize it if told that they did. I can see it clearly from reading various academic periodicals from the USA, especially those devoted to SF. By rote methodology, these poor university-housed academic souls blather, blabber, split hairs, and can't even see what kind of hairs these are, where they come from, and how much they're worth. The brief period of writing to these periodicals in order to put in my missionary-apostolic two cents is essentially behind me. Not worth the time and rhyme. I consider Todorov, e.g., to be a learned ass and his structuralist theories not worth a tinker's cuss, and I consider it to have been a

---

[63] Religious officials in ancient Rome who interpreted natural signs (especially the behaviour of birds) with a view to gods' (dis)approval of proposed action.

complete waste of time to enter the lists to prove that this is the case. Culture either proceeds by a slow process of self-cleansing, crystallization, clarification, stabilization (sort of like old wine), and then everything works more or less as it should, or else these automatic innovative-mutative processes become (like they do today) highly defective, inoperative, precipitating the emergence of cultural pathology which no single enunciation can affect in any way. I see around me a mind-vacuuming ice age — never mind what the would-be cultural periodicals say — while on the other side of the Big Water I see the flip side of this process: **permissive, conditioned chaos.** In this type of situation there's no point in looking for external road signs; instead, one must rely exclusively on oneself. I don't regard what I'm saying as especially pessimistic; to me this is only a diagnosis of the way things are, and nothing more.

[...]

****

Cracow, 23 April 1976

[...]

In terms of objective existence, information cannot (I think) be equal to matter (e.g., to stones or stars) because information always relates <u>to somebody</u> and comes into existence <u>due to somebody</u> (notwithstanding the fact that this "somebody" may be a bean or a bird — which is to say, a <u>species</u> of <u>natural evolution</u> — or a computer transmitting data to another computer; in this last case, the physical system of reference consists, of course, of people). Information is a state of a dynamic system — logically constrained and physically

embodied. Because of this, the entire hypothesis
as it is presented in "Donda"[64] cannot be taken
seriously. I could rework the hypothesis to enhance
the appearance of credibility but the more it would
gain in **plausibility,** the more it would lose in
simplicity, and I was after simplicity! "Donda" is
about a "forbidden road" that leads to scientific
discovery. Everything in it, that **"Lord's countdown
made the world"**, etc., is said by the nature
of things only playfully. After all, even Prof.
Donda does not believe that he really stumbled on
God's method of creation, even as he openly mocks
scientists who used to mock him. I thought I made
it very clear. In one word, the hypothesis is only
a narrative PRETEXT. I think this is allowed in a
story of this type. But even if we were to take
the hypothesis for a moment (ad usum delphini)
seriously, it still wouldn't entail anything in
terms of **Purpose, Sense, etc.** I can see here no
logically compelling argument for it, no connection.
Let's assume (this is going to be a highly fanciful
idea) that in the course of natural evolution there
arises a race of thinking beings whose brains are
constructed in such a way — from such molecules
— that, when an individual thinks of something
specific, as a result his brain begins to undergo a
violent process that leads to the brain's explosion
or to some other type of self-destruction. (Say,
for the sake of the argument, that in the course of
thinking the **pattern** generated by the processors of
the cerebral substratum attracts molecules of such
chemical composition that they initiate a chain
reaction: this is utterly improbable but physically
NOT IMPOSSIBLE). So what? Let's say that when such
a being thinks something "blasphemous" in terms
of their faith, just then — caused by that very
thought — the brain particles brought together in
this way "catch fire". "My judgments flashed like

---

[64] In Polish, "Professor A. Donda" appeared in *The Mask*; there is no English translation as the story was inexplicably left out of *Memoirs of a Space Traveler*.

lightning upon you". (And even if such a being could not have been created by natural evolution, it's always possible to <u>artificially</u> construct a being whose information processors consist of elements containing plutonium so that, in a given configuration, you get a nuclear ignition. Does anything follow from this in the "theodictic" sense? <u>In my opinion, nothing at all</u>; after all, you can always assume it was pure COINCIDENCE, with no para-physical import). Undoubtedly, the culture of such — e.g., robotic — beings might fashion a creed maintaining that this was "true blasphemy" and that explosions are "God's punishment", but as with every faith, even this would not have proven the existence of transcendence.

[...]

Today I got a letter from another <u>president</u>, Mr. Pohl from SFWA, who writes that SFWA members brought it to his attention that the SFWA statutes make no provisions for honorary membership, <u>eo ipso</u> Lem cannot hold this type of membership (although he has had for 2 years...). Isn't it droll? I must, however, craft a polite reply, reining in my delight for having been finally kicked out of this noble institution... In the Bavarian <u>Volkszeitung</u> a long article, asking with irritation why qualified institutions fail to nominate Lem for the Nobel Prize.

And yesterday I had a very unpleasant hour-long discussion with Ms. Director who came to see me from Warsaw with an idea for a big colourful Lem Show on TV (in September). They've invested so much labour into it already! Opening shot: sunrise, rooster crows from my roof but it's a <u>Robot</u>. Then you see Lem tying up fruit trees in the company of two more robots. Etc. Naturally, in no time you've got scantily dressed girls, navels flashing, dancing, jumping, thank goodness no one asked me to jump alongside the girls. With great difficulty but politely, all the same, I refused to agree to this idiocy and Ms. Director left deeply offended, convinced, I'm sure, that I'm not right in the head, that I think I'm God's Gift To The World since I don't want to participate in such splendid entertainment! As for me, I'm tired of all such buffoonery, to be honest. Due to, among other things, bad health, insomnia, etc.

[...]

****

Cracow, 15 May 1976

[...]

It is not true that, in order to create, one needs special comforts, preparations, material affluence, and the like. Dostoyevsky, not the worst writer in the world, is only one of many proofs a contrario. You write if only you can write and have something to say — and then you write day and night and evening, a day here, a day there, on dirty scraps, with a broken pencil, and when you get into it, nothing can stop you, not the death of those near you, not personal mishaps and tragedies, nothing, maybe except apoplexy or sudden death. Everything else that people say is bull.

[...]

Various ideas, some perhaps fertile, who the hell knows, maybe even sublime, clatter around my head but knowing how much effort, difficulty, drudgery, and concentration is involved in completing any project, I'm doing exactly nothing. It is very gloomy, this conviction after a great number of years as a writer that the loftiest qualities of one's work, the summits conquered at the highest cost, have essentially no serious TEMPORAL significance: for if, thanks to these sacrifices, the work will endure, by then the author will be in the grave. And what's the value of such dubious immortality?

[...]

****

Cracow, 16 June 1976

[...]

I lack the strength to lie to my boy, and now in his ninth year he can see that daddy doesn't go to church, and, asked about the beginning of creation, gives different answers from what they teach in religious classes... Truly I see no escape from the bind I'm in. Even if I decided to hold back, aware of extraordinary psychological benefits of faith, I still couldn't tell my child what I don't for a moment believe myself. Sooner or later he would sense it.

[...]

If I'm **out of joint with my time**, it is above all because no one today expects from literature any lessons, epiphanies, advice, teaching, in one word — apostolism. No one is interested in it. This type of approach to literature is regarded today as outdated, anachronistic, naive, silly, as presumptuously pretentious. I hear that I've been awarded a state prize for lifetime achievement... just when I'm so dissatisfied with my achievements. What strange accidentality, insouciance, and transience govern the fate of books — I mean, the ways in which they are received. Besides, dear Sir, there is also the nontrivial fact that I have been (or: am) a Godless apostle — that my casting about for this Being has all come to a sorry end, i.e. to nothingness, for only the circumstances of my casting about in my works were comical, and this vis comica[65] may sometimes obscure the deeper glumness...

[...]

PS. I think Carter will win the elections.

[...]

****

Cracow, 17 July 1976

[...]

I'm writing as a convalescent, following an operation I underwent on June 21st. There were two complications — first an inflammation of a vein in my right hand after an intravenous injection of a contrasting agent for urography — this meant that I could do practically no work after coming home, and then 16 days after the operation I suffered an internal haemorrhage, the clots from which blocked the bladder; after they had inserted the catheter, I was driven 100 kilometres back to Katowice for surgery because only they have the capacity to perform electro-resection of the prostate[66] (the doctors were unable to stem the bleeding at my place). I lost about half a litre of blood and this prolonged the convalescence so that now, even though I'm home and being "intensively fed", I'm still weak, albeit on my feet and without discomfort, slowly burrowing my way through a mountain of correspondence that has piled up in the meantime.

---

[65] Latin: "comic power".
[66] Transurethral electro-resection of the prostate (TURP) removes prostate tissue using minimally invasive surgical techniques.

[...]

It was a curious return from the eschatological domain to everyday mundanity, for over there — notwithstanding all the agonies, blood, etc., notwithstanding the enormous and terminal pressures — over there you come at least momentarily face to face with the meaning of life unrelated to anything else outside itself, and here I've got a pile of papers, letters, contracts, proofs that continue to look like stupid and superfluous banalities to me...

[...]

****

Cracow, 2 September 1976

[...]

Here is the secret. The style of The Cyberiad came about when I noticed how ORIGINAL and AMUSING were the shortcuts in which I jot down new ideas on scraps of paper — and how later on, when I sit down at the typewriter "for the gala performance" intended to "clean up" these notes and turn them into "literature", these same ideas morph into stiffly ironed formal sentences, so that in the end I simply started to plug these shortcuts wholehog into what I was writing; that's primo, and secundo — I began to give free rein to this "private", "unofficial" undercurrent in which my thoughts SPONTANEOUSLY flow into sentences and, having caught them "in the act", I'd put them on paper. I'm not saying that this is absolutely EVERYTHING that went into The Cyberiad, but that, even if this may seem prima facie a triviality, to me this rather naïve, almost self-evident realization, was a GENUINE DISCOVERY.

[...]

****

Cracow, 14 September 1976

[...]

NB., amusingly, there's a new book out in Germany that consists of several writers' UNWRITTEN works, those they had planned to bring into existence but for various reasons didn't, and it includes my contribution under the title of <u>Mr. F.</u> — this is a modern "Mr. Faust" — a story of a guy who falls in love with a woman who is no longer what she was (let's say that Marilyn Monroe was revived from attempted suicide, now she's around 58-60, a lonely, weird, aged, depressed and hysterical drug addict — but that, based on her photographs, films, the legend that trails behind her, a young man falls in love with her, and "abandons" himself to this woman; I made up the time and place where they could have met, and also explained why, in the end, I did NOT want this project to become a fully fledged work...)

[...]

****

Cracow, 18 September 1976

[...]

Recently I've been reading the third part of Bertrand Russell's autobiography and I got unspeakably disappointed and concerned by the intellectual decline of this wonderful old man who, in his dotage — he was 80 years old — got it into his head the addled idea that he should put all his efforts into saving Humanity from the atomic **"holocaust"**. As if he had forgotten about his theoretical knowledge that you cannot achieve anything sensible IN THIS WAY, and most certainly NOT the "Salvation of Humanity". Perhaps, indeed, because of senescence he had become incapable of intellectual work and perhaps his febrile comings and goings were but a ruse, an evasion, an escape into an "activist posture" that got between him and self-knowledge — auto-diagnosis — a spiritual death years ahead of physical death?? In any case, I read it with sadness, seeing how constrained this great intellect had become in the last phase of his life.

[...]

I feel at times that Carter may lose because, oddly enough, he is "too good" — that is, too intelligent. This is, no doubt, a handicap. (It's another thing that I can't fathom how a genuinely intelligent guy could wish to be president — whoever has any real brains is bound to give the Office a wide berth, knowing that too much in a presidency depends on blind fate and too little on personal talents). My Wife and I spent a few days in Zakopane, looking up in rain and fog our favourite spots, old mountain nooks and crannies. The construction boom is in full swing, the crowds are horrible, rusty cans and piles of garbage in what used to be secluded spots, it's all so sad, time to admit that the Tatras[67] I remember from the old days are no more and will never come back.

Physically I'm healthy, but I still don't feel like writing at all. How shall I put it? I've grown totally indifferent to readers: to people who might reach for my books. I realize how exceptional is a reader who understands what he's reading — and this knowledge depresses me! To recognize the aesthetic qualities of a work is not so difficult and not so rare, but to understand the author's ideas, even if they lie on the surface, without being veiled in

---

[67] Tatra Mountains in the south of Poland.

any way — to care for novel ideas, that is truly an extraordinary rarity.

There were more than 80,000 NEW titles displayed this year at the Frankfurt Book Fair. Something like 6,000 more than last year. Funny, isn't it? 80,000 authors, each with the Nobel Prize in his schoolbag, hoping for Fame and Fortune. 6 divisions of them, more or less. So much easier to be the son of a rich man or, failing that, of a dethroned king or of a guy who stole millions and cached them for his family!

[...]

****

Cracow, 30 September 1976

[...]

Who the hell knows why things ARE like this, but it's a fact — a fact inferred from 25 years of dealing with publishers (at this point, with publishers from all over the world) — that they have FUNDAMENTALLY NO CLUE about literature (and if not they, then the editors assigned to acquisition and the press readers, which in practice amounts to the same thing). Only rarely does anybody have a "nose" for books (I'd say that, in West Germany, Dr. Unseld from Suhrkamp Verlag had a "nose" for mine). They just don't have a clue, and that's it. So, to dream of a publisher who knows his job, who can spot diamonds in shards of glass, who is, moreover, patient, understanding, and doesn't keep a viper in the pocket where he keeps his money — who is maybe even a generous Maecenas of the arts — is to dream of a utopia. I'm not saying that such a publisher could <u>never</u> exist (today), only that I have never met one that would be so exceptionally excellent all around — you have my assurance on that, and

I've lost count how many I had dealt with from all those that published me. Globally, there must be at least about 100 (i.e., about a hundred bigger publishing firms in Europe and England; I had fewer contacts in America, just with Seabury — with Ace, Avon, and Walker on the outside looking in). NB., these are, above all, massive bureaucratic machines geared towards bulk printing and towards securing a return on their money, whether by pre-publication sales of supplementary rights or by fine-combing for bestselling authors. My knowledge of what goes on in the USA is enhanced by reading what various authors themselves have admitted in writing, from which I've learned that that the vast majority of serious writers, including Saul Bellow himself, have been supported by sometimes not that easily obtained stipends (Ford, Guggenheim), which means that not even their global renown guaranteed them a minimum salary sufficient to support a family at a level of an average-earning technician or engineer in Detroit.

[...]

****

Cracow, 30 September 1976[68]

[...]

I used to be a jack of all trades: I translated Russian books on feeding livestock, just to make a living; I was a gofer assistant at the Conservatory at the Jagiellonian U; I repaired German automobiles during the war (more often I wrecked them as much as possible); I was a (lousy) welder, a doctor, a critic, a columnist, an editor, an author of medical studies... yet I don't see any of these as a sheer

---

[68] Second letter from the same day.

waste of time. It all goes into storage somewhere inside. I also realize that life experience is essentially untransferable (literature may precisely be said to be an almost vain attempt to transfer personal experience by NONPROPOSITIONAL means).

[...]

Mrs. Ursula Le Guin wrote to me recently to say how embarrassed she was when I had been thrown out of SFWA, and how upset by what sundry SFictioneers had written about me in the SFWA Forum. I never read any of this stuff but, to be honest, I'm not bothered by it in the least since to me the opinion of morons is worth exactly nothing. (My reply to her was along these lines). I can't hide that I feel better after having been kicked out since I don't want to have ANYTHING to do with SF, and this honorary membership was, after all, a kind of connection.

[...]

****

Cracow, 28 October 1976

[...]

A priori my chances of surviving the war were minuscule, perhaps 1:1,000. This can be corroborated even mathematically, by establishing what percentage of, say, my ethnic bracket made it. The war not only made me independent, but took away all the control my parents had had over me before then. As for my metier, the stabilization of my fate — my parents, Father especially, wanted me to become a doctor (then referred to as a "free job"), so in September 1939 I was to enroll as a medical student. The fact that I continued my medical

studies after the war was partly because of inertia
— I'd had 2 years of med school in Lvov behind me
before the city was annexed into the USSR before it
was captured by the Germans — and partly because
I didn't know what to do with myself. When we
got repatriated to Cracow, I seriously considered
becoming a welder, that is, a skilled blue-collar
worker. But even though my father regarded with
quiet terror the fact that I'd have to abandon my
studies (I was nowhere near getting the diploma),
having experienced the war which had pulverized
any and all expectations of "stability" he didn't
even attempt to advise me, knowing that any advice
he could muster on the basis of the first part of
his life was practically useless. For a long time
I was quite literally a young fool: I couldn't take
advantage of my abilities, since I didn't know
myself what they were. I was 27 when I started
to write the first book of which I'm not ashamed,
Hospital of the Transfiguration. But even then I was
in danger of getting bogged down in tripe, vide:
The Astronauts.

[...]

Professor Hogarth from His Master's Voice is, in a
way, me; I also used to enjoy being mean to people,
and still have this reflex and probably will until I
die, but gradually I took to heart what I had read
in Einstein. He wasn't kind and generous to others
out of the goodness of his heart, but because he
had decided that "this was the right thing to do".
I can't say whether his confession was subjectively
honest. I can't even say if I'm being subjectively
honest in subscribing to his proclamation, but it
seems to me I am. I try to rein in my contempt
for others, I try not to stand in anybody's way if
I can avoid it, or if I think I can. Undoubtedly,
some motives behind ethically "lofty" behaviour can
also be low in nature. I couldn't wreak triumphant
revenge even if the right opportunity presented
itself because of what is probably a "low" reason:

ordinary cowardice in front of human misery. (I mean, you may crave evil, but you must still find the courage to inflict it, just like you must be bold enough to act out the erotic perversions you may harbour in your soul).

[...]

****

Cracow, 5 November 1976

[...]

I'm glad that Carter won, even though I could not rationalize my gladness. Ford's vapidity and low intelligence is a fact, but he had a sense of responsibility, and so ended up making few stupid errors. And Carter, if he's as smart as they say, may get us in trouble. In spite of this, I'm glad. This is connected, I think, as much to my "intelligence worship" as to my aversion to stupidity. **Your academic community**? Well. Perhaps one of my greater disappointments in terms of "professorial wisdom" was what happened with Science Fiction after American universities began to incorporate it into their study programs. As it turned out, it simply went through an "academic upgrade". My impression is that, <u>percentage</u>-wise, there are as few <u>intelligent</u> people of <u>principled</u> judgment and artistic <u>taste</u> in the **academic community** as in the general population. What is (in trace amount) "intelligent" in SF — a homeopathic dose of maybe 1:1,000 or even 1:10,000 — did NOT get recognized and brought to the limelight; instead, what is inferior and dumb gets dissected with solemn unction in professorial-doctoral essays, dissertations, and seminars as the writings of Authentically Great People. This, I think, was the last drop that filled my cup of dismay — I no longer want to have anything to do with SF, even as a critic.

I'm curious to see the reaction of Western Maoists to what's going on in China because the ultra-leftist circles in the West nourish a myth of the perfection of the Chinese state, a myth of happy Chinese as truly happy and free people, free within what is permitted and recommended by the Little Red Book, and now this myth is undergoing violent erosion as a consequence of what the Chinese themselves are up to. The entire exoticism, the enigma of perfection is disappearing and in its place you have the old, perfectly familiar arsenal of pragmatism and sociotechnic methods of totalitarianism.

[...]

****

Cracow, 12 November 1976

[...]

My attitude to the death of other people is, I would say, conditioned to a great degree by my experience under the occupation as well as by my medical studies, both of which are responsible for a certain mundanity with which I approach the symptomatology of agony, death, and the "natural history of corpses". I don't see my father's grave as a place that's dramatically important, that demands from me some kind of special devotion, visits, etc. Perhaps, if Father himself had selected the place under the big tree where he is laid to rest, or if he had at least known and seen it, I would have developed a connection between him and his grave, but he didn't know that place, never visited it in his life, and a dead person is one who is literally no more. Attachment to graves has always appeared to me an indecent cultural aberration, a kind of self-deception on the part of the living, an attempt to concretize what cannot be fundamentally in any material form concretized. It so happens that I have assisted during the agonies of strangers and of people close to me, and every time I only wished that they ended as quickly as possible.

Of course, even if such agonies don't always take the form of a kind of monumental <u>exertion</u>, a kind of highly intense struggle, it does happen often enough when a person is dying of "natural" causes, such as illness, rather than from a shot to the head. Then, under the automatic command of biology, the organism mobilizes these final, GIGANTIC physical reserves and throws them onto the table in a final bid, while any sufficiently knowledgeable person who comprehends the futility of these awful exertions (as doctors do) feels especially helpless — unless it happens to be the <u>treating</u> physician, who presses on with the treatment, smothering in this way the inner awareness that all this is completely in vain. Such actions on the doctor's part may be interpreted as pathetic or as dramatic in terms being faithful to the highest principles, to the very SENSE, of the medical profession — but, lying outside the outermost limit of sense, such actions can also be interpreted as highly <u>immoral</u>.

[...]

In my opinion, a corpse ought to be burned without any pomp and circumstance; it ought to be got rid of quietly and with shame. But this is only my cultural heresy.

[...]

****

Cracow, 3 December 1976

[...]

Just today I finished reading Bellow. Reading may be saying too much: I lasted about a hundred pages and only thumbed the rest. I wouldn't even have endured to a hundred had it not been for the recent verbal lashing I gave you for your quick, deprecating critical judgments precisely about Bellow, and if I hadn't seen the multitude of worshipful reviews of this utterly worthless book. I can't escape the feeling that Bellow wanted to write a bestseller, that this was his sole motive — but at the same time a bestseller that would not only get "legs" with the public, but also aspire to Higher Things. The raptures from the critics — not to mention the Swedish Academy — are an otherwise incomprehensible disgrace because the book is flat from the beginning to the end, contrived, trivial, and denunciatory. The denunciation, aimed at the Public, depicts a threadbare stereotype of the artist as an irresponsible lunatic and, at one and the same time, both trucks in this stereotype and explains it as the "spirit of the times", which supposedly precludes the presence of any other kind of Artist than the one for whom success is God (meaning, Fame and Fortune in Broadway theatres and by way of film scripts). Much less is said about the greatness of the works created by Messrs. Humboldt and Citrine than about the tit size of the ladies who gratified these Artists. To top it all, Humboldt's GRAND GIFT turns out to be a sketch for a script, presented in extensor,[69] from which you CERTAINLY couldn't make the hit film the producers salivate after. How disgusting, tasteless, gossipy, insignificant, unnecessary all this is — and how highly praised. One doesn't stand a chance with the kind of public and the kind of criticism that treat this book as Opus Magnum. Naturally, this doesn't change the fact

[69] Latin: "at full length".

that Bellow is the author of Mr Sammler's Planet and Henderson the Rain King. Even this year the New Yorker carried his two-part report from Israel, a good, solid, clear-toned piece of work; I can hardly believe he wrote it at the same time — the same man who created this drivel. With, to top it all, restatements, auto-plagiarism, of Mr. Sammler's Planet — unbearable!

[...]

****

Cracow, 28 December 1976

[...]

Me, I've got problems. The other day my wife came in and, seeing me strangely depressed, asked what it was, and I had to reveal with a certain embarrassment that I had just received a letter from Moscow from Prof. Shklovsky, a rather eminent astrophysicist, which contained the results of his latest research which concluded that humanity is unique in the Galaxy and perhaps even in the Metagalaxy, that we are Completely Alone... and this made me horribly sad, both for psychological reasons (since several years back this same Shklovsky professed the Multiplicity of Inhabited Worlds) as well as factual since, in the end, maybe there really isn't Anyone else — and this thought appeared horrible to me! I have to keep fending it off...

[...]

The statistical view of humankind is certainly pessimistic. Statistics appears to be the physical side of events — and today its flip side is Nihilism. Actually today there are two kinds of nihilism, Eastern and Western. The Western is the very "axiological implosion" of which I wrote more than once (other people too): the collapse of what used to be life's Imponderables, the belief in facilitating a snout-in-the-trough Spiffy-Lite Easy Life — Here — and Now — one consequence of which is an equation of Love and copulative marathons, of happiness and Piles of Money and Piles of Nice Expensive Things, etc. This is one type of nihilism, the one responsible for the fact that only the present counts, that politics is becoming short-sighted, that art and everything else is calculated for immediate effect; and as Dow Jones, unemployment, and inflation clamour for attention, things that decide our **to be or not to be** fade away from sight. This is nihilism of the open society (**Poppers open society**). And **in closed society** you have nihilism engendered by grinding society into a carpet of individuals by means of total disinformation, falsification of reality, authoritarian control using sociotechnic means — by technological decerebration (that's right), by dumbing down, and by producing 100% cynical attitudes as the only ones that "pay off" in this life. This is what the "convergence" of two forms of nihilism — neither of which has been sensu strictu Intended by Anyone — rooted in two different (so extremely different!!) social systems looks like. Vae Humanitati[70] — woe to the dolts who one way or the other let themselves be taken advantage of! At the bottom, both are different types of utopian undertakings — different roads but identical in their results — to build a Paradise on Earth.

[...]

****

---

[70] Latin: "woe to culture" (or: civilization).

Cracow, 26 January 1977

[...]

I have read Malamud, both <u>The Assistant</u> as well as the collection <u>Idiots First</u>, with something about Fidelman in it.[71] Naturally, I appreciate Malamud's class. There can be no doubt about the quality of what he writes. However, if you allow me a little fantasy, what if I saw a fairy who asked me if I wanted to write like Malamud does, if I wanted to "become" Malamud (the problem here, though, is that this proposed wish fulfilment hides a catch: given that Malamud writes like Malamud, whoever wrote exactly like him would necessarily have to be secondary by being <u>second</u>; this is the situation of an original artist like Vermeer and his genius imitator van Meegeren)? I'd tell the fairy no, I'm not interested. Why? Because <u>aut Caesar, aut nihil</u>.[72] Because I don't care to be <u>primus inter pares</u>[73] — I'd rather be <u>alienus</u>. Different, in the sense of trying to take literature beyond literature, toward, what? The future? Nonsense. Toward action, naturally. By this token, however, I want the impossible because literature does not act in the same manner that a shovel or a bomb does. Nevertheless, that's what I want. This madness has, of course, its glorious as well as monstrous antecedents. De Sade tried to take literature beyond literature in order to pounce on Culture, on all human Bodies and Souls, in order to break the bones of stars, derail planets from their orbits, he really desired all that. He knew, of course, that it was impossible and the whole tension in his writing comes from his very awareness of this impossibility. It is this impossibility that spurred him on the most, it helped him

---

[71] Malamud's collection *Pictures of Fidelman* reprints two Fidelman stories, "Still Life" and "Naked Nude", from *Idiots First*.
[72] Latin: "either Ceasar, or nothing" (meaning: all or nothing, going for broke).
[73] Latin: "first among equals".

articulate his vision (and, as an artist, he was talentless) most adroitly and most successfully. My own (stillborn) efforts aim at the almost direct reverse. Literature that explores Humankind from the inside, so to speak — literature that stops short of the limits of species-specific norms, instead of trying to break through them in a mad charge — literature that sounds out Humankind, exemplifies Humankind, pities Humankind, literature flagellating Humankind, understanding Humankind, forgiving it and not forgiving — all this is not enough for me. What handicaps my efforts from the get-go is that I don't place chance in the fates of individual lives so much as see it as an overlord permanently leaning over the planetary cradle of life, over the emergence of the human body and mind; seeing the adventitiousness of evolutionary, cosmic, adaptive accidents that created us, and not believing in any Creator, and as such being unable to hold Anyone accountable for all these eons of creation, my diatribes cannot even hope for a vector, for an ultimate Addressee — I cannot even count on his being, unbeknownst to me, Somewhere Out There. There is no one like Him left for me. My stance, which generally undermines the significance of the exquisite artistry of writers like Malamud has, of course, nothing to do with envy, derision, or with elevating myself. The goals I set before myself were simply different, and I can only note that I'm cognizant of the extent to which the political misery in which I'm up to my ears over here had contributed to my radicalism, also in literature. Not a small part of my intellectual toils were devoted precisely to ridding myself of this misery. But the impetus stayed with me as a kind of surplus. As an East European, I know as well as one can only know the hardness of stone, the look of furniture, the odours of flowers and manure, the extraordinary fragility of culture, its total reversibility, its momentary, unstable, continuously eroded existence, and this knowledge never really leaves me for a moment. For this reason, I and every other thinking person in these parts regard your so-called problems as childish, problems of a child whose gleaming toy car runs a little awry. I'm watching your ballet on the frozen surface of a lake, your reluctance to reflect on the abyss that yawns underneath the ice on which you perform these exquisite pirouettes. Your worries that the skates are not sharp enough, that the ice is not slippery enough, that your acrobatics are not always as magnificent as you would wish — I compare these worries against the magnitude of the iced-over abyss; meanwhile, when your artists and thinkers speak of this abyss at all, it is mostly in ludic terms which no one ever really takes in deadly earnest — even they themselves often just <u>play</u> around with this self-proclaimed Apocalypse which for us is already stale, old bread with an all too familiar taste.

[...]

****

Cracow, 1 March 1977

[...]

I'm always bemused by the tenacity with which scientists attach themselves to the latest results of their research, treating them as the definitive pieces of the puzzle from which a few may, perhaps, be still missing but with the overall design showing through. After 30–50 years it turns out that the whole puzzle has to be reassembled from scratch all over again when new pieces are discovered that could never be fitted into a coherent whole with those from the existing pattern. I've got no proof for this, except induction from the past, from the history of science, but I'm certain that it's going to

be the same with genetic engineering. We have
identified the DNA alphabet and we're under the
impression that we're very close to understanding
the mechanisms of ontogenesis (embryogenesis,
etc.). This is analogous to learning the writing
alphabet in the conviction that this will lead
in no time to the production of works as good
as Shakespeare's. Actually I think that things
are simpler in the latter case than in genetic
engineering. What appears to be the greatest threat
today will in the end prove marginal and of little
consequence, whereas things we hardly expect will
expose the limits of our ignorance (which is twice
as bad, because it's a different story <u>to know what
one doesn't know</u> than not to even know <u>what</u> one
is ignorant of, given that in the former case you
can — and in the latter you can't — ask sensible
questions of Nature by means of experiments).

Israel has joined the ranks of my book
publishers.

[...]

****

Berlin, 5 April 1977

[...]

My acquaintances over here bring me up to date
on the shabbiness of political entanglements,
Western corruption, persecution of the Left, and
my soul is in pain for, hating communism, I see
at the same time that there is no attractive
alternative for other-thinking individuals in
the **welfare state** BESIDE IT. And this doubles my
solitude, knowing the subtle distaste with which
even intelligent people here react to our (visitors
from the East's) "ultraconservative" views, which
are no more than a result of boundless nausea with,

disillusionment in, and distrust of the intentions of Eurocommunism...

[...]

****

Berlin, 18 April 1977

[...]

The difference between the East and West today is, if I can put it like this, that the West tolerates everything (that's why it can tolerate Lem as well). Why not, since everything is so "permissive"? Compromises... pluralism. Of course, this is <u>better</u> than concrete cellars, NKVD,[74] faces smashed to a pulp, lies at every step, and a slow but steady favouritism of scumbags over those who are honest. But what does that have to do with anything? My freedom is internal, it must be internal to begin with because, if I'm not free inside, the only way I can externalize it by selecting a **pocket ass-hole** over Venus. The West really is in bad shape, but in my eyes it is certainly and incomparably better than the East. <u>You don't seriously think it could be otherwise?</u> Say, one country permits eating little children right before the eyes of crazed mothers, and another permits eating <u>absolutely anything</u>, whereupon it turns out that the majority of people in that country eat shit. So what, does the fact that most people eat shit demonstrate — if anyone were even to take it seriously — that it is <u>better</u> to eat children alive?

[...]

****

[74] Russian: National Commissariat for Internal Affairs, precursor to KGB.

Berlin, 6 May 1977

[...]

Essentially everything that needed to be said about the Soviets has been said and published many times over, with detailed precision. Naturally, the books I'm reading here are those I can't get hold of in Poland; among others, personal memoirs of the Germans (mainly from Pomorze[75] — Pommern) over whom the Red Army avalanche rolled over in the year of Hitler's defeat, 1945. The notes of a certain physician (a Count, by the way), a man of faith who survived this hell, who witnessed everything that the Russians, manufactured by their monstrous system, were capable of — many times his memoirs expressed my own opinions and judgments which I had never put to paper. (Even though I hadn't witnessed the things he had). The cruelty of the Germans occupying countries under Hitler is, along the entire length of the spectrum and in the entire breadth of experience <u>incomparably different</u> from that of the Soviets. The Germans — let's do the banal part first — were methodical planners, followed orders in a rather impersonal and mechanical manner; they regarded themselves as a Superior Race, and us, Jews, as <u>Ungeziefer</u>,[76] as worms to be exterminated, worms SO cunning, so full of chutzpah that, thanks to this rascally mimicry, they <u>dared</u> to assume an illusory semblance to Humanity. The Russians, on the other hand, were a horde conscious of their inferiority in a wordless, deaf sort of way that goaded them to any-and-all licentiousness, raping 80-year old grannies, dishing out death indifferently, superficially, in passing; demolishing, wrecking, destroying all signs of prosperity, order, and civilizational wealth, while displaying in the disinterestedness of this destruction a high measure of Inventiveness,

---

[75] Pomerania, north-central province of Poland.
[76] German: "vermin".

Initiative, Attention, Concentration, Intensity of Will — as such they weren't taking revenge for what the Germans (NOT THE SAME ONES, anyway!) had done to them in Russia but, rather, they were wreaking revenge on the world outside the borders of their prison — the basest kind of revenge possible since they shat on everything. No animal exhibits such — how shall I put it — EXCREMENTAL DETERMINATION as the Russians did, overfilling with their excrement smashed up salons, hospital wards, bidets, bathrooms, shitting on books, carpets, altars; shitting with joy on the entire world just because they COULD trample it, crush it, shit on it, and then for a good measure rape and murder (they raped women who had just given birth, women convalescing from major surgeries, women lying in puddles of blood, they raped and shat; and they just HAD TO have stolen watches, so much so that, if some poor little soldier boy missed out, just because others had stolen everything there was to steal from a German hospital, he would CRY in his misery, even while yelling that, if they didn't immediately get him a WATCH, he would shoot three people). Once in Moscow in the sixties, it was after midnight, I went straight from the airport to a restaurant in an "exclusive hotel" (in the street, the crowd eager to PARTY, kept pounding in vain on the hotel gates), and even though no one there raped, murdered, or shat, it was THE SAME THING, and it made on me an indelible impression, this raging horde deprived of faith in God — i.e., I saw people robbed of Values, people with amputated ethics. It was an incredibly disgusting spectacle.

    These stories, these diagnoses, are not new but our civilization does everything it can to conceal, tread on, bury, overlook these things, to walk away from them and, if it's not possible, to **EXPLAIN AWAY**. The Soviet system, as a "corruptio optimi pessima",[77] is de facto a system of breeding all the traits of which debased Man is only

---

[77] Latin: "corruption of the best is worst".

capable. (Betrayal of those held dearest, sending friends to torture, mendacity at every step, life of falsehood from cradle to grave, stomping on traditional cultural values while setting other cultural values in concrete — for, clearly, all this rape, murder, and shit is but one side of the coin, while the other is Soviet puritanical Victorianism, "nationhood", "patriotism", "communist morality", etc. What is there to say, to add, to all this! And, to a radical non-believer like me, the thought that, even though there is no God, there PROBABLY is Satan BECAUSE there are Soviets — this downright obsessive thought cannot but keep coming back. A superpower with a falsified ideology (no one believes in it), falsified culture, music, literature, education, social life — everything falsified from A to Z so thoroughly, under such a weight of repression, under such police surveillance, that you cannot but contemplate the thought: who is this for, if not for the Lord of the Flies??? I know he doesn't exist — but in SOME WAYS this lack of the Negative Pole of Transcendence makes this diagnosis even worse.

[...]

****

Berlin, 7 May 1977

[...]

What surprises me, what (to be honest) I myself don't understand, is my ability to anticipate certain lines of development of scientific thought — me, who am after all an amateur and, at best, a well-rounded dilettante. I'm inclined to think that my analyses are generally grounded in concepts from natural evolution, with "accident", "stochastics", and "chance" interpreted in biological and not straightforwardly physical terms. How else could

I explain that, writing Summa 14 years ago, I recognized the then hot issue of "artificial intelligence" — approached as a magnification and amelioration of HUMAN intellectual capacity, as an imitation of HUMAN mind (brain) — as a "myth", as a common type of mistake in cybernetics?

[...]

(In my opinion, and it's an opinion for which I have NO evidence as such, the picture of the brain currently gaining ground among specialists — that of Two Halves complementing each other, with the left hemisphere controlling the "logic of discrete steps" and the right the "intuition of leaps and bounds that integrate data by para- or metalogical means" — ISN'T correct. The unvoiced premise in this picture is STILL the sui generis perfection of the brain, that is, the assumption that the brain is built in this "yin-yang", "hemi-complementary" way because THIS was the optimal solution to the problem of creating a "mind of a thinking being". I, on the other hand, think it was what the Germans call Aus einer Not eine Tugend machen.[78] Our brains have excess capacity not in the sense that already the Neanderthals bore future-oriented capabilities (and thanks to this futuristic potential, i.e., thanks to this "anticipatory construction", our brains manage to cope with the demands of our civilization); their excess capacity is much more "shoddy". It is as if we had a wheelbarrow, a car, a crane, and a spade at our disposal and had to limit ourselves only to their combinations when working out solutions to emerging problems — I'm trying to say that the brain's surplus capacity is partly "redundant" and partly even "detrimental" from the point of view maximizing human intelligence. We're not thinking with the best equipment there is, but with what is only "so-so" — with what the evolutionary process stuffed into our heads, cobbling it together

---

[78] Latin: "making a virtue out of necessity".

out of successes and errors, out of felicitous factors and retarding ones). The way I see it, you can't "recreate the brain" not because this is an outrageously difficult task owing to the PERFECTION of the original but because it's very difficult to include in this "perfect imitation" the sum total of the <u>accidental factors</u> that had shaped it. The task, in other words, is not of the logico-deductive type; rather, it is a search for the countless circumstances and paths through which the process of anthropogenesis crawled, erred, stumbled, and then <u>partially</u> rectified these stumbles... this is why I continue to maintain that you CANNOT recreate the human brain and that it's going to be easier to create <u>sui generis</u> my Golem, i.e., a system that LACKS the mental make-up of humanoid minds.

[...]

****

Berlin, 29 July 1977

[...]

I came across fragments of a book by an eminent Soviet logician and philosopher, Zinovev (not the Zinovev slaughtered by Stalin but a different one), who wrote an apocrypha depicting the Soviet reality in the light of his very intense, ice-cold, and intelligent logical analysis, and I can't say that there was anything new there for me except for a concise accusation <u>cum</u> diagnosis that Zinovev directs at the Soviet people — no other dissident ever has dared to articulate this truth SO unrelentingly before — that in some way the people CRAVE the bondage of the Soviet regime, that they relish their enslavement, that they enjoy the servitude because they Love their Shackles.

[...]

****

Berlin, 13 August 1977

[...]

There must be a number of reasons behind my massive lack of enthusiasm to write anything important, anything serious, here in Berlin. Some of them are uninteresting, others banal, trivially straightforward ("Guy has written himself out"). I don't know, maybe it's indeed so. But maybe it's something else. Inside the cage that is Poland or any other "socialist country", in this artificial coercive system, one can dream of Freedom (of speech, art, thought) and, as such, come to believe that "if only it weren't for Them — ha! we would have great art and culture and PEOPLE WOULD FLOCK TO WHAT WRITERS CREATE". But over here, where the "initial and boundary conditions" are already more or less optimally in place, you can see what happens instead. If you put the fistful of fame or popularity I've earned in Poland under a magnifying glass and critically evaluate its chemical composition — this is like hacking off a limb on which I'm sitting, but I'll say it all the same — my editions in the "socialist countries", my popularity, the breadth of my resonance owes directly, among others, to that LACK of freedom, understood as <u>freedom TOWARD something</u> and not just <u>freedom FROM</u>.

[...]

****

Berlin, 28 August 1977

[...]

I have just read Roth's Portnoy's Complaint; have you? This is a kind of Bellow shifted on the visual spectrum towards obscenity and comedy, but, in the end, it's the same thing, only having undergone a complex transformation, just as if somebody performed Beethoven's Fifth (but masterfully, a virtuoso!) on a comb with a toilet bowl for percussion.

[...]

Right now I don't feel any yen to write philosophy. My Credo, simplified and compressed, is as follows: Everything, practically everything that is revelatory, wise, and original, that ultimately explains the Wretchedness and the Loftiness of human existence, has Already been SAID at one time or another, in most cases only to vanish without a trace — in part in the cesspools that today's mass culture brings with so much effort to orgiastic explosions. Sperm, shit, tears, blood have drowned out all the big words. And to write more of them, only to see them drown like all the others, would be, before anything else, Very Stupid. And wisdom that conducts itself stupidly is not a pleasant sight.

[...]

****

Cracow, 19 October 1977

[...]

I think I understand it better now than ever before how dangerous it is for our species to court

catastrophe by chasing illusory goals such as
perfect collective happiness, perfect justice, and
other perfections. I also understand it better than
before that we are created to inhabit the moderate
zone in EVERYTHING: both the lack and the excess of
freedom destroy and paralyze us equally and with
equally terrible results, even if these results
are, naturally, different in either of these extreme
cases. No, we don't need too many degrees of freedom
nor their utter lack. By the same token, even though
society needs faith, the latter should neither be
too exalted nor too cynical, not too high and not
too low; it shouldn't demand sacrifices that are too
high, but neither should it demand virtually <u>nothing</u>
at all; things are worst when faith turns out to
be either a total vacuum behind a façade riddled
with holes, or else a façade which hides the police.
If our species survives our age, it will certainly
be known as the age of social engineering and not
as the age of astronautics or cybernetics, because
it is social engineering that poses the greatest
hazards on the path embarked on by <u>Homo sapiens</u>...
And even though I don't see writing ABOUT IT as the
chief duty of all writers, I do see it as their duty
to know ABOUT IT.

[...]

****

Cracow, 4 November 1977

[...]

I've often been asked in interviews which of my
books I value the most, and (not knowing the answer
myself) I used to say: <u>Solaris</u>. Now I realize (it's
very funny that it's happened only now and so
suddenly) that the criterion for the answer must be
the desire to reach for my own books, and once I had

realized it I could see that I never read <u>Solaris</u>.
But I do from time to time read <u>The Cyberiad</u> and
<u>The Star Diaries</u>, although, since they had appeared
in your translation, no longer in the original but
always in English.

[...]

I learned that my article on SF in the <u>Frankfurter
Allgemeine Zeitung</u> — the translation of which had
caused the firestorm of ill-will and my ouster from
SFWA — had been abbreviated by some 25% in the
translation, replacing my moderate terminology
with insults and adding the subtitle: "the world's
worst literature". Funny to see this xenophobia,
this small, dirty meanness coming from people
who write about the Cosmos, Cosmic Civilizations,
All Cultures, of the world, of the times, etc.! I
couldn't give a flying kite about the whole thing
but, still, it's sad somehow.

[...]

****

Cracow, 16 February 1978

[...]

Lem's Three Laws proclaim: 1) nobody reads anything;
2) if they read, they don't understand anything; 3)
if they read and understand, they instantly forget.

[...]

****

Cracow, 23 February 1978

[...]

Just today I prepared a concise English text to be used as a template for replies to a mass of letters — and there is a mass of them — waiting for me: invitations to a SF Con in Metz in France, from a publisher in Helsinki, from the Bulgarian Academy, from pollsters, from guys editing SF Encyclopedias and other such like baloney, not to forget prayerful requests from Sweden and who the hell knows where else for autographs. There are at least 20 URGENT requests for those at the moment, e.g., a director of the Modern Museum in Stockholm had a brainstorm to ask ME to write a preface to their catalogue and sent me a bunch of albums with sculptures that HE associates with <u>Solaris</u>. Then there is East German TV, West German TV, <u>Der Spiegel</u>, etc., etc. My wife's character is not armoured heavily enough to shield me effectively from all this, not to even mention that she and Tomasz had both been down with a flu for a damn long time now. (Someone must get groceries, though, and this someone is me, plus I had bought my wife a car (our second) to give her more flexibility, so now with two cars, sick family, and an 85-year old mother who is barely hanging on, it's time to call for God's Mercy rather than think about holidays). Escape, yes, but where to? I see now how stupidly I frittered away my Berlin holidays, I could have gotten some work done but, no, I wanted to show off my business muscle to the capitalist world, haggling out DM30,000 for a TV show, I wanted to lecture at the Freie Universität, attend book launches here and there in East Berlin, and the precious time slipped through my fingers.

[...]

Books, i.e., author's copies from Greece, Spain, Russia, Holland, are swelling in my cellar, no more room for all of them. A guy who "did" his doctorate on me has mailed me his dissertation angling for a personal opinion; yesterday, they take me aside at the Jagiellonian U to tell me that they're trying to rustle up an honorary doctorate, and what do I have to say to that? Rarely now do I find time to write to old friends. SFWA is inquiring through third parties if I'm still pissed off by the Boot in the Rear. I'm going to stop this list here, it's getting too long and boring. My income more or less doubles every year, and though I'm still far from being a multi-millionaire, I can already <u>taste</u> more or less what "brilliant Career" is all about.

[...]

****

Cracow, 2 April 1978

[...]

After the war, in 1945-1947 my father supported me, then a 26-year old, in my medical studies; that was the time when I began to earn a living (very modestly, at first) with a pen. I actually felt that what I was doing was not quite right, writing all kinds of sensational trash for the cheapo monthly booklets put out by private publishing houses that were in business then — one of them was "Every Week a Novel", and they paid me (pretty well, considering the times) for these stories. I was pretty keen on shoring up the home budget since my father (born in 1879) was already 68 and still carrying all of us <u>all by himself</u>. I also wrote and published poetry (in the <u>Popular Weekly</u>) but all that was peanuts, and not too often, either. I was even thinking of writing under a pseudonym, but in the end decided against it since it wasn't "right" to do (write) something and not admit to it! You gotta have some courage and sign your own name. That's how I saw it.

I don't know myself how many — 3, 4, maybe even 5 — of such "Novels Every Week" I managed to sell then, giving the money to my father (my needs at that time were strangely minimal). I actually think that the fact that my name began to appear THERE didn't serve me right, because it sticks to you (this kind of rep) for a long time, but I had no idea about the consequences. This is a bit funny, but I know that some Polish readers bemoaned the fact that, in the later years, I would not allow these sensational stories to be published in book form! Because they liked THEM so much...

[...]

****

Schladming, 16 July 1978

[...]

PS. Goddamn ty pewriter "stutters", what a piece of crap, doesn't even have the exclamation mark without which NOTHING at all can be expressed*!!*

[...]

****

Cracow, 11 October 1978

[...]

As for catastrophe theory, I know it (so long as nobody asks me questions about it). It started to make waves some three years ago but, almost as fast as it rose to acclaim, critical voices began to charge that much of it didn't hold water. I don't worry in the least about us being suddenly thrown in disarray by the nature of the world, so perfidiously put together as to make further progress of knowledge impossible. On the other hand, I was quite perturbed by the results of last year's computer modelling of planetogenesis, insofar as they concluded that Earth was an exception, that the relevant processes must thread so many eyes of needles, like a slalom, without lethal disturbances before life can arise and develop over a few billion years, from which it can be inferred that we are a two-headed calf of the Galaxy — maybe even, God forbid, of the Cosmos. It's not about looking for company in other galaxies, you understand, but about a total <u>reordering</u> of a worldview, were it to be better and better confirmed that we're stuck in this curious Cosmos like a single toe in a gigantic boot...

[...]

****

Cracow, 24 January 1979

[...]

PS. To me, Malamud and not Singer ought to have got the Nobel Prize.

[...]

****

Cracow, 8 March 1979

[...]

At first I wrote Golem's Second Lecture "About Itself", put it aside to cool off, and all of a sudden found myself writing a review of a book that does not exist, but ought to. Die Endlösung als Erlösung — from the pen of a German professor from Göttingen — subtitled "The History of Genocide". No two ways about it: the subject is not just overdone, but overdone to death. But I got tempted by a new take on Endlösung der Judenfrage,[79] the perfidy of which lies in that it is a GERMAN who writes my book and I'm merely reviewing it. The whole thing is pretty extensive, and I was myself surprised by the argumentative conclusions. I've had a few positive responses at this point. I'll probably publish it in Germany first, just to make them sweat a little. It's okay, insofar as I learned this year that I'm the highest-selling author at Insal-Suhrkamp. So, since they air-lifted me onto a high pedestal, in the spirit of justice I'll drop that pedestal straight on them.

[...]

****

Cracow, 13 July 1979

[...]

In A Perfect Vacuum I mocked (in some respects) Finnegans Wake, trying to show that even the greatest talent who creates a work of such a degree of complexity that not even a hundred Talmudists

---

[79] German: "final solution to the Jewish problem"; Lem is speaking here about *Provocation*.

could grasp it in the entirety of its manifold radiative meanings ultimately <u>creates a flop</u>, because literary works are created for normal (or even genius) readers but not for code-breakers — and if a work IS aimed at a tiny handful of extraordinarily percipient individuals endowed with a capacity equal to the author's to unravel these codes, even then I've got doubts about the sense of creating such a work — and this is exactly the reason, by the way, why I hid the newly finished lecture by Golem (on mathematics) in the drawer, since even the devil himself couldn't follow it the way I would have liked as the author. (From which it follows that it's possible to create books that will be **too sophisticated** in the sense of being TOO accomplished, TOO refined compositionally, TOO excellent: in short, EXCESSIVELY original.)

[...]

****

Cracow-Berlin, 10 April 1980

[...]

I had an idea of writing summaries of books that ought to be published but aren't. I wrote the first one IN LIEU OF a German anthropologist. It's a "thick two-volume" work about the Nazi genocide. The first volume is called <u>Die Endlösung als Erlösung</u> and the second <u>Fremdkörper Tod</u>.[80] My thesis revolves around a (half-fantastic) historiographic hypothesis — in brief: that death, which constituted an irreducible part of culture during the middle ages, is now "alienated", lying in the street, so to say, and nobody in this materialistic, hedonistic, technological, and perfectionistic

---

[80] *The Final Solution as Redemption* and *Death As Foreign Body,* respectively.

civilization knows what to do with it. The book employs terms like "the place of death in culture", "re-utilization of death". The entire first volume is about the Judeocidal crime, about the deep secret motivation behind it — it's really difficult to summarize it, so let me only say that it is written with complete seriousness and not ironically, like in A Perfect Vacuum (it comes up to some 40 pages in my "summary" review). I know the Holocaust first-hand, hence I made all efforts to ground the whole thing in factual events in order to reveal this crime as the first act of "re-utilization" of death on a massive scale — there is a lot in there on the ethics of evil, etc. The thesis is that first the Nazis needed to invent an "embodiment of universal evil", so they picked the Jews; later on, in the age of subcultures ushered in by the continued collapse of internalized norms, perpetration of death was taken over by terrorism as a way of self-affirmation and group identification; sectarian suicide is the final step on this road. Initially only the state was "permitted" to kill and only the state held the right to select victims; then terrorists sought these "rights" by targeting representatives of the state, like in Italy or Germany; finally, "everyone is guilty of evil": acts of group suicide close the circle. What I'm going to do with it, I don't know yet myself.

[...]

****

Berlin, 19 October 1982

[...]

I have received two propositions, one from German TV and the other from German radio. Some guy wrote an utterly idiotic show based on one of Ijon Tichy's voyages: if I accept his screenplay, I'll get around 3,000 dollars; another guy wants to put me between Hermann Kahn and some German SF writer in a series of lectures on utopia: here, if I agree to say things I don't even believe, I'll get about 1,500. I declined both offers. I think — I'm saying "I think" just to be cautious — that I would have rejected them even if I had been dying of hunger which, NB., is far from the case.

[...]

****

Vienna, 5 September 1985

[...]

I think I well understand your reservations about calling the computer — GOD.[81] Whereas in Polish it's simply a matter of it sounding FOREIGN, in English it would be wrong and out of place. As a first and not the best equivalent, I'm thinking of the German GOTT. I don't know how to say God in Swedish or in any other Scandinavian language. An ALLUSION to the English word would be, I think, welcome. LORD seems to me too vague, not to mention that it has other, rather undesirable connotations (of a MASTER who rules). DIEU is probably too far, too much of a stretch. I thought of ADONAI, or JAHVE, but associations with the Old Testament also seem to me undesirable. How about deforming the word GOD, so that it still sounds similar (e.g., GODD)? This is a very fine question of stylistic taste, and I have a feeling that, rooted in English, you'll find it easier to assess the correctness or incorrectness of

---

[81] The matter concerns the translation of a name of onboard computer in *Fiasco*: it was eventually rendered as DEUS.

this change. The last resort would be leaving GOD for the time being and looking for a better idea in the course of the translation. Let me add, by the way, that I had the greatest difficulties with the titles to almost all of my books, so that many of them aren't even mine; e.g., the German Also Sprach Golem[82] was invented by Dr. Rottensteiner in a take on Nietzsche, very appropriately, I think. In short, I confess my incapacity.

About the ending. The actions of the protagonist are not fully rational; the way I see it, he neither intended to be sent on a one-way suicidal mission nor was in a position, after the landing, to coldly calculate his chances and, as such, the chances of the whole mission. I can vouch that he didn't understand the situation because THE ENDING was a surprise even for me. Let me put it like this: on the final pages the plot carried me in the direction I had not anticipated, in the direction of such utter alienness and "otherness" of the planetary intelligence that it makes all debates, all moral discussions on the Hermes[83] misdirected, for it turns out that the "Others" are far more alien than any human being could have expected. Neither the "hard", "power" approach (forcing "contact" by blackmail) nor strategies rooted in the Gospels are of any use. Nobody in the human crew is right: neither the "doves", with Father Arago in the lead, nor the "hawks". And, in the critical moment, the protagonist behaves exactly like you described it in the blurb to the publisher. His accumulated frustration finds a release in an idiotic, desperate, and essentially senseless act. "He did see the Quintans", as he had been promised on the Eurydice, but he saw SUCH Quintans as no human beings could wish to

---

[82] *Thus Spoke Golem*, second edition of Bereś's *Conversations with Stanislaw Lem*.

[83] A scaled down version of the mothership *Eurydice*; in the novel *Eurydice* takes astronauts across space and *Hermes* completes the journey by bringing part of the crew to the vicinity of planet Quinta.

see. Intelligent mould? Some form of a colony of sentient quasi-insects or microbes? No idea, but it's something that a human cannot internally agree with. NB., opening fire, the Hermes had no intention to kill its own envoy, aiming at aerials outside the area that had been agreed as open to exploration. No one on the Hermes could know that laser strikes would hit the man they had sent down. To me the situation was symmetrical: the Quintans were as alien and "other" to humans as we were to them, with the proviso that, thanks to the "pictorial story" broadcast to them, the Quintans — they can be putatively envisioned as gigantic, intelligent, antagonistic anthills — knew something of human appearance and by that token knew that the kind of "contact and understanding" sought by the humans was unrealizable. So, even as they were loath to accede to the ship's landing for strategic-pragmatic reasons that had been taken into account by the Hermes, on top of this they were aware of the futility of this expedition, mission, endeavour, and conceded to it only under the threat of death.

To make a long story short, the envoy got himself into a situation from which there was no "winning" way out, only he refused to accept it and attributed to the Quintans intentions which most likely they didn't have, but in any case did not have to have (intentions of concealment, camouflage, deception). In this type of situation, the psychological reaction of the protagonist seems to me quite plausible: he was not capable of letting go of all the anthropomorphic illusions that the human mind willy-nilly attaches to the concept of a "technologically highly developed civilization". The fact that this civilization is itself trapped by its own military technology is a separate point and something of a red herring: identicalness and universalism of Nature's character assumes, after all — at least to me — a similarity of technological formations developed by beings arbitrarily different in their history, physiology, and anatomy, and THIS similarity of the fruits of technology in a way forces humans (also on board of the Hermes) to take it as a given that, if technologies are similar, their creators must be similar too. The ending reveals that this assumption was wrong.

You are right, of course, to regard the whole story as a kind of allegorical prognosis of relations on Earth; it could be a model of these relations, although not a model that corresponds one-to-one to the "Earthly original", but rather one that has its own, different characteristics. I hope I managed to convey to you the conceptual background behind Fiasco. (NB., the story about the Crystal Ball was introduced on purpose, it's a kind of allusion to the futility of the expedition which, after conquering the greatest obstacles, achieves precisely NOTHING).

[...]

****

Vienna, 20 November 1986

[...]

We're doing so-so here. I've been ill now and then; ain't no way you can count me among bullish, hale old men. Worse, perhaps, after having written Fiasco, I tried to take a breather by reading some of the latest books that made the top grade in the world. The Name of the Rose, yes, indeed; my wife and I also enjoyed Isaac Singer, but beside these two a strange vacuum! And especially in the domain of **hard core SF**. This is droll, but conforms to the Law of Symmetry: I cannot stand American SF (guys like Asimov, Disch, and all the rest), whereas they in turn find me indigestible. At the same time there are Dissertations written about me in the US! Your remarks about Fiasco were exceptionally accurate: I wrote it in the state of extreme depression (collapse of Poland, my departure, illnesses, major surgeries whose outcomes could not be predicted, responsibility for changing my son's life trajectory). As for the sexual symbolism — I don't know WHAT exactly you're talking about (it's not that I have objections against this type of symbolism in a book — I know <u>nothing</u> about it naturally, it's just that, having looked at the text from this angle, I couldn't see anything of this sort).[84]

[...]

Have you read my <u>Provocation</u>, a 50-page fictive review of a fictive two-volume study by a fictive German anthropologist on the subject of the Holocaust? It's interesting that I wrote this apocryphal review so well, that, unwittingly, I fooled professional Polish historians who attempted to order my nonexistent study from Germany — while in Germany <u>itself</u> my book received not <u>one</u> review after it had been published! As far as I know, my publisher made sure that the book was unavailable in any bookstore, with the result that, if you were really determined to get hold of it, you had to xerox a library copy... in Austria and Switzerland, on the other hand, there was no resistance and reviews did come out. Germans are horrendously guilty of what they've done to us and, deep inside, these superdemocrats realize it perfectly well!

[...]

****

---

[84] See Swirski, *The Art and Science of Stanislaw Lem* (2006) and *Stanislaw Lem* (2015).

Vienna, 15 January 1987

[...]

As for Sagan, I picked up the German version of his book — for which he got, as you must know, an advance of a MILLION dollars — I looked it over in a bookstore, even though I heard only bad things about it from physicists over here. Alas, they were right, I'm sorry to say. You know I love science (especially **hard science**), but he really ought to change his name to Vaselini Asstrotten: his President of the US is a woman, the protagonist is also a woman — no one, with me in the lead, will ever charge Sagan with the terrible sin of sexism.[85] The sin of lack of imagination is less important. There is NOTHING in this book to "grab" me in the least, and I must second Dr Rottensteiner who, in his fanzine Quarber Merkur (editions of 400 copies) ripped into Sagan — which, NB., won't hurt Sagan in the last... Boy, this thing is really bad. Intellectual values are not incompatible with aesthetic values; if they were, there would be no criteria in PURE mathematics to decide what's WORTH doing and what isn't. His discussion of God would do credit to boys graduating from Highschool, never mind today but even 50 years ago, when I was in highschool myself. **Wormholes** are a totally skewed idea, physically it's a complete fiction; anyway, it's not that important whether this thing is realizable or not, only how it all hangs together as LITERARY FICTION. The quality of the latter is decided on the basis of the HUMAN WORLD depicted in a book, and his Soviet Russia is painted with icing sugar, it's just a shame. Makes me sad to talk about it, since this is a symptom of the overall situation in mass culture. Recently I read Pynchon's Gravity's Rainbow, an utterly demented dud. I think, if someone were ready to invest $1,000,000 in publicity, you could make a bestseller out of an old phone book.

[85] Carl Sagan, *Contact* (1985).

[...]

After _Fiasco_ I have not written anything, I'm not counting articles; alas, I think what you wrote about _Fiasco_ was bull's eye since, indeed, I did have a deep feeling that it was my swan song, maybe because during the last three years I had had three operations, had half of my entrails removed, had been writing in between hospital beds, so not exactly in the best of moods. Strangely, some people say that _Fiasco_ is very interesting and good, others say that, although good, it makes high demands on WESTERN readers, these fusspots who should be given only what's already pre-chewed, God forbid that it should demand THINKING and, worse even, that there was PHILOSOPHY in it, unless of course it's at the eight-grade level, i.e. the level of Sagan's theological disputes...

[...]

Stanislaw Lem Chronology

1921	Born in Lemberg, Poland, now part of Ukraine.
1931	Finishes elementary school.
1939	High school matriculation.
1940	Begins medical studies at Lvov's Medical Institute.
1940–44	Wartime occupation by Nazi troops.
1944	Resumes interrupted medical studies.
1946	Family repatriated to Cracow, Poland, where Lem continues medical studies. First novel, *Man From Mars*, published in a Cracow weekly.
1948	Completes studies; does not take capping exams for fear of being drafted into the army. Publishes numerous stories and essays. Editor of a popular science magazine.
1948	Commences work as a research assistant at Science Study Conservatory at Cracow's Jagiellonian University.
1951	First science-fiction novel in book form, *Astronauci*.
1953	Marries Barbara Leśniak.
1955	Publishes a realistic and a science-fiction novel. Receives Golden Cross of Achievement.
1957	Volume of nonfiction on cybernetics and politics, *Dialogi*. Receives literary award from the city of Cracow.
1959	Publishes *Eden*, *The Investigation*, and a short story collection. Awarded one of Poland's highest cultural awards.
1961	*Annus mirabilis*: publishes four books, including *Return from the Stars*, *Memoirs Found in a Bathtub*, *The Book of Robots*, and the acclaimed *Solaris*.
1961–68	"Golden period" in Lem's career: multiple novels, collections of stories and essays, volumes of philosophy and criticism, and *Summa technologiae*.
1968	Son, Tomasz, born.
1971	Several novels and story collections, including *The Futurological Congress* and the groundbreaking *A Perfect Vacuum*. Receives multiple national and international awards.

1971	Invited to present a paper at the first SETI scientific conference. Joins POLAND 2000, think-tank of the Polish Academy of Science.
1972	Andrei Tarkovsky's film *Solaris* triumphs at the Cannes festival.
1972–82	Multiple belletristic publications, including the popular *Chain of Chance* and the experimental *Imaginary Magnitude*, as well as philosophy, ethics, futurology, criticism, radio scripts, polemical writing. In the wake of multiple appearances on radio and television, Lem becomes a national spokesman on cultural, literary, and popular scientific matters. Nominations for the Nobel Prize in Literature.
1976	Notorious ouster from the Science Fiction Writers of America.
1981	Honorary doctorate from Wrocław Technical University.
1982–88	Emigrates from Poland; takes up residence for one year in West Berlin, then Vienna.
1985	Receives Austrian State Award for Culture.
1986	Completes *Fiasco*, last work of fiction. Recipient of multiple national and international awards and distinctions.
1988	Returns to Poland, devotes himself to nonfiction.
1998	Honorary doctorates from Lvov's National Medical University, Warsaw University, Opole University, and the Jagiellonian University.
2002	Hollywood's blockbuster production of *Solaris*.
2003	Honorary doctorate awarded from University of Alberta, Canada; withdrawn when Lem unable to receive it in person.
2006	Dies on 26 March; buried at the Salwatorski Cemetery in Cracow.

Index of Names and Titles

1984, 20, 24

"A Good Shellacking", 34
A Cold, 113
A Perfect Vacuum, 1, 7, 64, 77–78, 87, 106, 109, 155, 157, 165
A Stanislaw Lem Reader, 1
Abernathy, Robert, 88
Absalom, Absalom!, 40,
Arabian Nights (see *One Thousand and One Nights*), 83
Arendt, Hannah, 32, 49, 68
"Apropos of the Wet Snow", 40
Asimov, Isaac, 5–6, 161
Astronauci, 165

Baloyne (character), 19, 28
Bellow, Saul, 39, 128, 134–135, 148
Beethoven, van Ludwig, 148
Beres, Stanisław, 159
Bloom, Leopold (character), 63
Błoński, Jan, 19
Borges, Jorge Luis, 1
Borowski, Tadeusz, 40–41
Brod, Max, 30

Calvino, Italo, 5
Carter, Jimmy, 123, 126, 131
Cat's Cradle, 29
Chesterton, Gilbert Keith, 11
Choynowski, Mieczysław, 86
Citrine, Charlie (character), 134
"Confession" (see *The Mask*), 65
Contact, 163
Cosmicomics, 5
Culture, 83

d'Estaing, Valéry Giscard, 98
Daedalus, 96
Darkness at Noon, 69, 115
Darwin, Charles, 64, 82–83, 109
Death As Foreign Body, 156
de Gaulle, Charles, 97
de Sade, Marquis Donatien Alphonse François, 20, 23, 28, 137
Dedalus, Stephen (character), 63
Demolitians (characters), 12
Der Spiegel, 151
DEUS (character), 158
Dialogi, 165
Dialogues, 12
Die Englösung als Erlösung, 155–156
Disch, Thomas M., 161
Doctor Faustus, 32
Dostoyevsky, Fyodor, 6, 12, 26, 39–40, 59–60, 63, 76, 111, 121
"Dragons of Probability", 62, 80
Dumas, Alexandre *père*, 17

Eden, 78, 115, 165
Eichmann in Jerusalem: a Report on the Banality of Evil, 33, 49
Eichmann, Rudolf, 33, 68
Einstein, Albert, 6, 19, 29, 82, 130
Electrodicy, 87
Extelopedia, 45

Father Arago (character), 24, 159
Father Brown (character), 11
Father Orfini (character), 78
Faulkner, William, 3, 40
Fiasco, 1, 24, 158, 161, 163–164, 166

Fidelman, Arthur (character), 137
Figaro, 96
Finnegans Wake, 155
Ford, Gerald, 83, 98, 128, 131
Forster, Ian, 63
Frankfurter Allgemeine Zeitung, 114, 150
Fremdkörper Tod, 156
From Lowbrow to Nobrow, 113

God and Golem Inc., 78
Golem (character), 39, 43–47, 65, 78, 146, 155–156
Golem XIV, 6
Gombrowicz, Witold, 14, 30, 39, 51–52, 108
Gomułka, Władysław, 74
Gravity's Rainbow, 163
Gregory, Lt. (character), 77

Hamlet (character), 30
Harey/Rheya (character), 65
Hegel, Georg Wilhelm Friedrich, 116
Heidegger, Martin, 31
Henderson the Rain King, 39, 135
Heraclitus, 44
Highcastle: A Remembrance, 85, 107
His Master's Voice, 8, 18, 42, 107, 130
Hitler, Adolf, 50, 67, 142
Hogarth, Peter (character), 18–19, 107, 130
Hospital of the Transfiguration, 130
"How the World Was Saved", 62

Idiots First, 137
Illusions of Grandeur (see Imaginary Magnitude), 37, 45, 78
Imaginary Magnitude (see Illusions of Grandeur), 1, 37–38, 41, 43–44, 62, 64, 74, 77–78, 87, 98, 106, 109, 115, 166
"In the Penal Colony", 30, 32
International Herald Tribune, 52, 54
Ivansky (Mr.), 102

Jesus Christ, 24, 27
Jack the Ripper, 68
John the Baptist, 8
Journal de Genève, 54
Journal of Abnormal and Social Psychology, 66
Joyce, James, 63

K. (character), 33
Kafka, Franz, 14, 22–23, 26, 30–33, 106, 108
Kahn, Hermann, 158
Kandel, Michael, 1, 37
Kashenblade, Commanderal (character), 21
Katar, 113
Ketterer, David, 71
Klapaucius (character), 34–35
Koestler, Arthur, 69, 115
Kultura (Magazine), 65

Le Bon, Gustave, 93
"Lecture XLIII—About Itself", 65, 155
Le Guin Ursula, 49, 129
Le Monde, 52, 83, 96
Lem, Stanislaw, 16, 20, 24–25, 33, 37, 39, 40, 44, 58, 66, 81, 84, 114–115, 155, 159
Lem, Tomasz, 151, 165
Leśniak, Barbara, 165
Levi-Strauss, Claude, 7
Literary Gazette, 84
Literature, Analytically Speaking: Explorations in the Theory of Interpretation, Analytic Aesthetics and Evolution, 13
Liza (character), 40

Machiavelli, Niccolò, 20, 27
Malamud, Bernard, 137–138, 154
Man from Mars, 165
Mann, Thomas, 14, 32, 103
Mao, Zedong (Maoism), 132
Marx, Karl, 116
McLuhan, Marshall, 83

INDEX OF NAMES AND TITLES

Memoirs Found in a Bathtub, 17, 20, 24, 33, 44, 78, 83, 109, 165
Memoirs of a Space Traveler, 119
"Metafuturological Conclusion", 78
Milgram, Stanley, 66
Mohammed (Prophet), 8,
Monroe, Marilyn, 125
Mortal Engines, 64–65
Mr. F. (Mr. Faust), 125
Mr. Sammler's Planet, 39, 135
Musil, Robert, 103
Mróz, Daniel, 58, 90

"Naked Nude", 137
Nature, 79
New York Herald Tribune, 83
New Yorker, 96, 135
Newsweek, 52, 54, 84, 96
Nixon, Richard, 48, 53, 55, 83
Nobel Prize, 14, 43, 73–74, 120, 127, 154, 165
Notes from the Underground, 40, 59
Nudelman, Rafail, 77

O'Brien (character), 20, 24–25
Obedience to Authority: An Experimental View, 66
One Human Minute, 2
One Thousand and One Nights, 62
Open Society and Its Enemies, 116
Orwell, George, 20, 23–24, 26–27, 34

Paris Match, 97
Pascal, Blaise, 32
Passage to India, 63
Peace on Earth, 1
Philosophical Studies, 62
Pictures of Fidelman, 137
Pilate, Pontius, 68
Pirx the Pilot (character), 38
Plato, 116
Playboy, 41, 97, 116
Podhoretz, Norman, 32–33, 68
Pohl, Frederik, 120
Popper, Karl, 116, 136

Popular Weekly, 152
Portnoy's Complaint, 148
"Professor A. Donda", 119
Provocation, 155, 162
Pugg, Pirate (character), 48
Pynchon, Thomas, 163

Quarber Merkur, 163
Quintans (characters), 159–160

Rabelais, François, 83
Radio im Amerikanischen Sektor (RIAS), 88
Rappaport, Saul (character), 19, 42
Ready, Helen, 44
Reston, James, 83
Return from the Stars, 77–78, 102, 115, 165
Rheya (character—see Harey), 65
Rilke, Rainer Maria, 15
Robotic Fables, 17, 64, 87, 107
Rorschach, Hermann (Test), 9
Roth, Philip, 148
Rottensteiner, Franz, 114–115, 159, 163
Runny Nose, 113
Russell, Bertrand, 106, 125

Sagan, Carl, 162–164
Sartoris, 40
Science Fiction and Futurology, 6–7, 78
Science Fiction Writers of America (SFWA), 47, 114–115, 120, 129, 150, 152, 166
Science News, 79
Science-Fiction Studies, 88
SFWA (see Science Fiction Writers of America)
Shakespeare, William, 94, 140
Shklovsky, Iosif S., 135
Sienkiewicz, Henryk, 17
Silverberg, Robert, 60, 64
Simenon, Georges, 106
Singer, Isaac Bashevis, 154, 161
Smith, Winston, 20

Solaris, 43, 64–65, 71, 77–78, 81, 89, 106–108, 111, 149–151, 165–166
Sorokin, Pitirim, 94
Spengler, Oswald, 94
Stalin, Joseph, 20, 23–24, 26, 146
Stanislaw Lem, 162
Steelypips (characters), 17
"Still Life", 137
Sturgeon, Theodore, 115
Suchodolski, Bogdan, 78
Süddeutsche Zeitung, 54, 97
Summa technologiae, 5, 49, 54, 79, 92, 107, 165
Swift, Jonathan, 10, 108
Swirski, Peter, 5, 13, 113, 162
Szpilki, 54

"Tale of the Three Storytelling Machines of King Genius", 16
Tarkovsky, Andrei, 166
The Art and Science of Stanislaw Lem, 1, 162
The Assistant, 137
The Astronauts, 130
The Book of Robots, 165
The Castle, 30, 32
The Chain of Chance, 113–114
The Cyberiad, 1, 15–17, 34, 48–49, 58, 62, 64, 80, 83, 87, 90–92, 102, 106–108, 124, 150
"The Errant Error", 39
The Exorcist, 60
"The Fifth Sally(A)", 17
The Final Solution as Redemption, 156
The Futurological Congress, 54, 59, 88, 165
"The History of Genocide", 155
The God That Failed, 115
The Investigation, 77, 165
The Invincible, 43–44
The Limits of Growth, 53–54
"The Man Who Was Thursday", 11
The Mask, 24, 28, 65, 78, 81, 119
"The New Cosmogony", 78

The Name of the Rose, 161
The Origins of Totalitarianism, 49
The Philosophy of Chance, 6–7, 9, 12, 32, 49, 79, 112
"The Second Sally, or the offer of King Krool", 35
"The Sixth Sally", 48
The Star Diaries, 6, 64, 79, 88, 106, 115, 150
The Sydney Morning Herald, 83
The Trial, 22, 26, 30, 32–33
The Underground Man (character), 12
Theodicy, 87
Thus Spoke Golem, 159
Tichy, Ijon (character), 10, 12, 38, 78, 88, 158
Time (magazine), 52, 54
This Way for the Gas, Ladies and Gentlemen, 41
Todorov, Tzvetan, 88, 117
Toynbee, Arnold Joseph, 94
Tristan and Isolde, 16
Truman, Harry, 55
Trurl (character), 35
Tryon, Edward P., 79
"Twenty-First Voyage", 6, 12

Ulysses, 63
Unseld, Siegfried, 127

Volkszeitung, 120
Von Humboldt, Fleisher (character), 134
Vonnegut, Kurt, 29

War of the World, 44
Wells, H.G. (Herbert George), 44
Wielopolski, Aleksander, 84
Wiener, Norbert, 78
William, Noonan, 83

Zimmermann-Göllheim, Irmtraud, 1
Zinovev, Aleksandr A., 146
Zipperupus (character), 16